Homes for the Future

Glasgow 1999
UK City of
Architecture
and Design

Published on behalf of Glasgow 1999: UK City of Architecture and Design, by:

August
116–120 Golden Lane
London EC1Y OTL
+44 171 689 4400
mail@augustmedia.co.uk

This book was designed, edited and published by August Media Ltd

ISBN: 1 902 854 02 0

Photography:
David Churchill; pages 5, 18–19, 28–31, 38, 40, 42, 44, 46 (small photo), 47, 48, 50, 52 (interior), 53, 55–58, 60–66, 69–74, 76–77, 79–85, 87, 88, 90–93
Phil Sayer, pages 2–3

Cover photographs:
© David Churchill

Picture acknowledgement:
Page 9 © Stadtarchiv Stuttgart
Page 11 © Mitchell Library
Pages 14, 15 © Royal Commission on the Ancient and Historic Monuments of Scotland
Pages 16, 17 Courtesy of Elder & Cannon
Page 43 Courtesy of Ushida Findlay

Series editor: Sarah Gaventa, Communications Director, Glasgow 1999
Editor: Nick Barley
Art director: Stephen Coates
Designer: Anne Odling-Smee
Copy editors: Ally Ireson, Jessica Lack, Alex Stetter

Contributors:
Ranald MacInnes
Naomi Stungo
Texts © the authors

Production co-ordinated by:
Uwe Kraus GmbH
Printed in Italy by Musumeci

Developing Glasgow's Homes

Deyan Sudjic
Director, Glasgow 1999

Glasgow Green isn't exactly where the city began; the dumpy gothic spire of the city's cathedral and the rough stone of the Provand's Lordship, the city's oldest house, marks that particular spot. But it's not far away: the High Street straggles down the hill toward the Clyde and the Green. It was the city's first public space, a safety valve for the tightly packed closes of the old town, somewhere to escape to for pleasure, and for dissent. A real urban space.

And it was here that the wealthy built their homes at the end of the 18th century, fuelled by the profits of the trade with America, and the Industrial Revolution. This was the precursor of the booming Pacific Rim cities, the Shanghai or the Hong Kong of its day, where the population doubled every generation, and the ambitious and the dispossessed flocked to make their way.

Glasgow Green was the victim of a move to the west by the business people who had created the city's wealth. It became the site of a clothes market (left), and a popular area for demonstrations.

Just as Glasgow was once the world's first industrial city, now it is one of the cities that has pioneered post-industrial regeneration. And Glasgow Green is the focus of an ambitious attempt to bring life back into the city. As one of the highlights of Glasgow's year as the UK City of Architecture and Design in 1999, the Homes for the Future scheme has seen the completion of 100 apartments designed by seven architects from around the world, a mix of social housing, private development, and publicly-supported projects, some designed to make home ownership more widely available to those on limited incomes.

The area has suffered from almost 100 years of continual westward drift, and the city has redefined itself in the process. Charlotte Street was once an elegant, gated community of classical mansions. It was where David Dale, the enlightened millionaire who conceived of the utopian settlement of New Lanark, lived. Until very recently, it barely existed as a street at all. A few steps away on the Green itself, James Watt is said to have hit on the idea of the steam-powered engine. But the noxious fallout of industrialisation, the leather works and engineering plants, drove out the very entrepreneurs who had made fortunes building them. If Glasgow is Britain's most American city, with its grid and its swaggering stone buildings, Glasgow Green was its South Bronx for a while. The wealthy abandoned it as soon as they could, leaving behind dereliction and decay. This is the fault line between the solidity of the city's dense urban core, and the shapeless sprawl of the housing projects of the East End, filled by the flea market of the Barras, and scarred by the barricaded pubs and the few remaining shops that are the legacy of the city's so-called height reduction programme. The tenements that once lined the arterial roads here were cut down to single-storey relics, as Glasgow briefly gave up the struggle to be urban.

By the middle of the 1990s, Glasgow Green was a place in which the past survived only as a series of hulks, their edges lapped by a sea of dereliction. The ancient baroque church of St Andrews, the Templeton Carpet Factory, and the former school on Greendyke Street, designed by Gillespie, Kidd and Coia (now the headquarters of the Wise Group which trains the long-term unemployed for the evolving job market), are all that survive in a lost urban landscape. The point of the Homes for the Future project is to give a new sense of identity and life to the area, to bring people back into the city centre, as well as to experiment with new forms of architecture. And it comes at the same time as the rebuilding of St Andrews Square, and a Heritage Lottery-supported scheme for the renewal of Glasgow Green itself.

This is not of course the first time that architecture has formed the subject of a permanent exhibition: it's a tradition that goes back at least as far as the Stuttgart Weissenhofsiedlung of the 1920s. What Glasgow wanted to do right from the start of the project was to balance the ambitions of a short-term exhibition with the long-term future of the area. This will, primarily, be a place to live, but it is also about encouraging architectural innovation. The site opened to the public in the very week that Richard Rogers launched the report of the Urban Task Force. And it is a pointer to how the ambitions of the government to encourage the regeneration of Britain's city centres can be achieved. This is not a suburb, but a piece of urban development.

Architecturally, the scheme has a strong sense of place, achieved even though it involves a wide variety of architectural approaches and backgrounds. It is Ushida Findlay's first European project, as well as the first major piece of work to be completed by the newly established Glasgow practice of McKeown Alexander. There is Ian Ritchie's copper-faced steel frame development for the Thenew Housing Association, as well as Wren Rutherford's careful exploration of the Scottish vernacular for Mactaggart and Mickel. There is RMJM's work for the young developer Joe Logan, as well as Elder & Cannon and Rick Mather's bravura penthouse apartments for John Dickie.

The project addresses the edge of Glasgow Green with a suitably urban scale, but it does not form a solid wall, as if it were some defensive enclave it offers views of the Green to its interior, and encourages visitors with glimpses of the rich variety of spaces behind the impressive scale of the main frontage.

While the urban tissue of Glasgow Green is scarred and battered, there were still clues that survived to provide a starting point on which to base an approach to rebuilding the area. First the Green itself, still a handsome space, offering sweeping south-facing views, in which the remaining towers of the Gorbals just across the Clyde form the middle ground towards an open outlook that is framed by hills and open countryside. It was obviously the greatest asset for the site. Then there were the two surviving buildings that bookend the site: Gillespie, Kidd and Coia's grey brick and expressed concrete-framed school from the 1960s to the east, and the red sandstone Hide, Skin and Tallow building at the west end of the site. They are buildings a century apart, in completely different materials, and informed by a vastly different view of the world. But both nevertheless maintain a certain scale and bulk that clearly speaks of city not of suburb.

It was clear that the blocks facing toward the Green would match this scale, and that there might even be an opportunity for one element to go a little higher as a landmark, drawing attention to the main way into the centre of the site. Odile Decq and Ushida Findlay both came up with solutions for this building. In the event, the Ushida Findlay scheme was selected.

Within the centre of the development, the intention was to offer a visual link with the Green beyond, but also to create an urban space with a coherence and identity of its own. A space that would not be a self-contained and entirely closed internal courtyard but one which would also offer the possibility of a route through it to the world beyond. Thus, the plan allowed for the inclusion of a second landmark structure at the northern end which could be read from Glasgow Green as the termination point of a route through the site. It is an arrangement that helps to reinforce the sense that this is not an enclave of new construction within a run-down area, but is a project which embraces its setting. On the other hand, the Homes for the Future site is substantial enough to achieve a critical mass, and to form part of a continuous chain of new building and refurbishment which ties the area back to the heart of Glasgow.

Homes for the Future draws on a number of key historical precedents. Among them, perhaps the most important is the Weissenhofsiedlung in Stuttgart. Masterplanned by Mies van der Rohe, it was subsequently used as a political weapon against immigrants by the Nazis in a supposedly satirical postcard.

The idea of co-operation between architects is always one which sounds attractive in principle but which is rarely achieved in practice. In this project it has been achieved with the lightest of touches. Every architect collaborated to submit a single planning application. There were discussions about a palette of materials, about the relationship of one block to the next, and of the way in which aspects of the development would be seen in relationship to others.

It means that there is a set of shared assumptions, but still latitude for each architect to use their own language. It has created a dynamic massing that embraces timber facing and white render, engineering brick and copper cladding. Each element within the overall development is clearly coherent in its own terms, but it also forms part of a larger composition, tied together by some large gestures such as the high-level walkway overlooking the Green, and the dialogue between the choppy rhythm of the curved mesh balconies that adorn the Rick Mather building and the smooth tight radial curves of the Ushida Findlay building.

The development is very much a three-dimensional composition, not just one which addresses the obvious presence of the Green, but also provides presence to the west where it forms part of the backdrop to St Andrew's Square, and on the north, where McKeown Alexander's point block establishes a gateway presence.

Homes for the Future was a project that depended for its success on the participation of many different people and organisations: Glasgow's planners, roads department and building control, Scottish Homes, the private developers who took on much of the risk, the masterplanners at Page and Park, the project managers at Rock DCM – led by Norrie Innes – and also Eleanor McAllister, Glasgow 1999's Depute Director; without such a successful collaboration, the project would never have been completed in the amazingly short time it has taken – just eight months on-site. Best of all, the project doesn't stop with the first phase: there are two more sites to come.

Housing in Glasgow

Glasgow has reinvented and rebuilt itself many times, developing a unique approach to housing in the process. Ranald MacInnes explores the city's housing history, from the tenement to the high rise.

The grid which forms the streets of central Glasgow (right) is unique in Britain. Its structure may be reminiscent of American cities such as Chicago and San Francisco, but the tenement housing which lines the streets is a form which the city has made its own.

In Andrew O'Hagan's novel *Our Fathers*, the main character is 'Councillor Bawn', a socialist housing crusader. In one of the desperate letters sent to him by his constituents, Bawn is urged to "demolish all the prefabs and get on with the high flats. To hell with the gardens. Homes are all that matters here. Let us see action in 1968 and for God's sake let the mothers have peace of mind with a decent home." The character is clearly based on David Gibson, Glasgow's messianic high-riser, but the year is way out. By 1968, serious doubts had already been raised about the city's incredible building programme.

Glasgow's astonishing energy, generated in the mid-19th century, was channelled by systems of strict planning controls into the creation of a monumental city of tenements, schools, libraries, public baths and even dance halls. When the City Chambers were begun in 1883, Glasgow was already on its fourth administrative office within living memory. The city had grown rapidly and it was now the most important example of 'civic improvement' in the UK. Glasgow had become a kind of 'city state' with a huge range of public services from water to street lighting and health, during the important phase of capitalist paternalism ironically dubbed 'municipal socialism'. The wealth created was spent lavishly on massive infrastructural and socio-cultural improvements. These are the roots of the City Corporation's effortless move into mass housing. This was a collective city, renewed and rebuilt time and again.

Although the City Improvement Trust had laid out areas of 'improved' tenements, speculators had largely provided Glasgow's housing, whether for rent in tenements or for sale in terraces and villas. Due to Scotland's historically tenement-dominated housing style, working class people were very rarely housed in Coronation Street-style terraces. Almost everywhere else, the word 'tenement' has a resonance of poor quality and cramped conditions. New York's tenement house museum, for example, is a one-room, windowless hell-hole. Many visitors to the National Trust's 'tenement house' in Garnethill, Glasgow, are surprised to find a spacious and bright flat. The reality is that the tenement is capable of subtle gradations in quality from a 'single end' (a one-room flat) to a 'mansion flat'. However, the tenement is much more flexible than the house: it can accommodate shops, offices, nurseries, and large and small flats, all in one building. In this respect, the modern tenement is the ideal vehicle for urban regeneration.

But the tenement has not had it all its own way. As early as the 1820s, a new trend towards the establishment of the villa as a principal residence of middle-class owners had already taken hold. Later, with improved transport by land and sea, especially through the railways, suburban villas were laid out on increasingly large and regularised patterns of streets. David Rhind's West Pollokshields layout, for example, was leased out in 1851 and a very large number of suburban villas were built. Alexander Thomson designed several villas in the area as 'one-offs' for relatively wealthy clients, but the majority of the houses used expensive materials within generally formulaic elevations. However, at the edge of Pollokshields, developers put up high-class

JOIN TO-DAY

John Dickie and fellow Homes for the Future developer Mactaggart and Mickel, are now building housing in central Glasgow, but in the 1930s, both companies were extolling the virtues of the suburbs in their press advertising and concentrating on out-of-town developments.

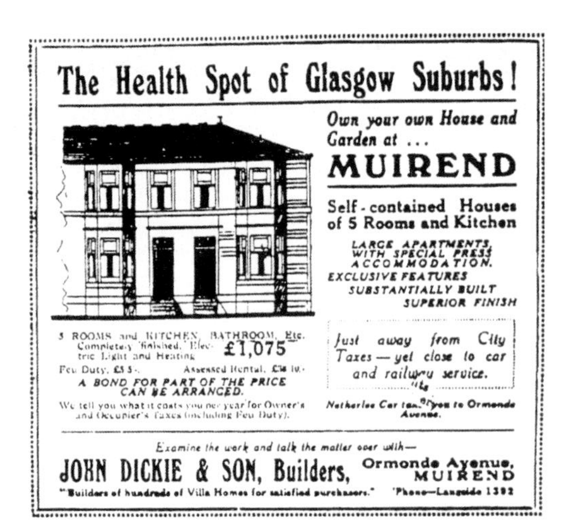

tenements, graded in status according to position.

The reputation of the tenement as a fit dwelling for the middle classes suffered marginally with the building of massive new districts of working class tenements, which were simply scaled-down versions of prestige models. However, developers did not abandon the middle class tenement. On the contrary, they built ever more grandiose examples, complete with maid's rooms, pantries and basement laundries. One example in the West End even offered telephones on each level, but for all the 'luxurious' devices employed, the building type remained essentially the same. It was the First World War which seemed to kill off the middle class tenement. Afterwards and until the 1980s, terraced townhouses, bungalows, detached houses or 'luxury' flats on the outskirts of the city were the preferred option.

Glasgow's tenements ranged from plain, affordable housing to prestigious developments with servants' quarters. It was only after the First World War that they came to be perceived as purely working class housing. As construction site from 1913 shows, they were built without the benefit of scaffolding.

Reaching for the sky

In the aftermath of the Second World War, Glasgow's 'can-do' political culture was well equipped to deal with the continuing housing problem. Earlier attempts to deal with the slums now seemed piecemeal. Rehousing efforts had continued throughout the latter part of the 19th century but even large schemes, like those of the Glasgow City Improvement Trust, which demolished all that was left of the medieval town and replaced it with working class housing, were less motivated by rehousing than clearance for its own sake. It was not until the post-war period that slum clearance began to be matched by the rehousing of those it displaced. For the most part, the horrific problems of Glasgow's slums had previously been shifted from area to area: to Gorbals or Garngad in the North; and a series of reports continued to highlight Glasgow as the 'cancer of Empire'. The Corporation now produced a scheme for an almost completely rebuilt 'healthy and beautiful city'. The City Engineer, Robert Bruce, prepared the plan between 1944 and 1945. The bold idea was to sweep away the slums and to replace them with relatively low-density, up-market flats of a type pioneered at Moss Heights in the south of the city. New garden suburbs would be built on the city's edge, and a daringly modern inner ring road was to be driven around its centre.

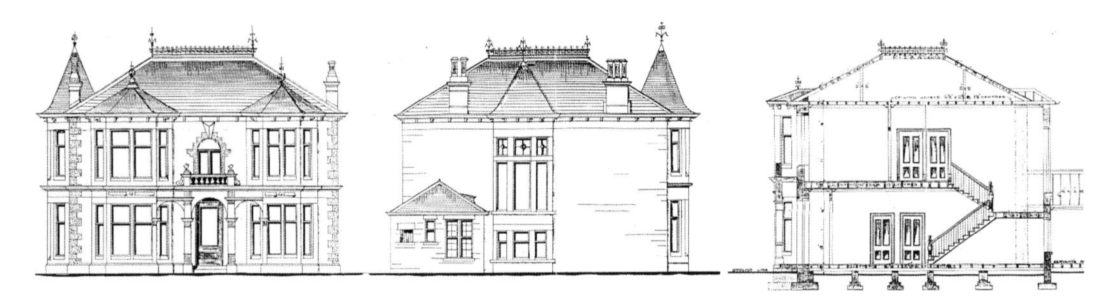

While tenements fulfilled the housing needs of thousands of Glaswegians, by the mid-19th century the first middle class buyers were choosing to move to the generous villas, like these, being built in suburban areas like Pollokshields and beyond.

The threat to Glasgow's programme came from an even more ambitious polity – the state. The Scottish Office dismissed the Bruce plan as a 'fantasy'. Their solution was to depopulate the 'congested' city of Glasgow. The Clyde Valley Regional Plan would have rehoused a quarter of a million Glaswegians in New Towns whilst preventing the further growth of the city by means of an encircling 'green belt'. The city was furious. Loss of population meant loss of political prestige. A compromise was agreed whereby swathes of green belt were conceded to Glasgow in exchange for moving 100,000 of its residents out. The garden suburbs planned for the periphery were dropped in favour of higher-density tenement developments at Drumchapel, Easterhouse and Castlemilk. Later, as Glasgow ran out of building land within its boundaries, the City decided that the only way was up. Seduced by the Modernist glamour of prestige tower blocks and pressed into urgent action by the continuing housing crisis, Glasgow built more high rise flats than any other city in Europe, including those in the communist bloc.

At first, tall blocks were put up as part of 'mixed developments' (low and high rise) in some of the 29 CDAs (Comprehensive Development Areas) identified as containing the worst slums. The most significant of these, because of its historic reputation, was Hutchesontown/Gorbals, and this work was allocated to some well-respected architects. One site (Area A, 1956) was rebuilt using four-storey, tenement-scale maisonettes; Area B was allocated to Sir Robert Matthew (1958–64); Area C to Sir Basil Spence (1960–66); and Area D (1961–68) to the experimental state agency, the Scottish Special Housing Association. Matthew designed 18-storey towers and lower blocks laid out on a north-south axis, entirely disregarding existing street alignments. Spence's controversial and subsequently dramatically destroyed development at 'Hutchie C' included large flats raised up on sublime Corbusian piloti (stilts): a "monumental tenement run mad" according to the *Architectural Review* of November 1967. The large flats had enormous balconies, the size of small gardens. This was to be a garden suburb in the sky. "When all the washing is out," said Spence, "it will be like a great ship in full sail". On the ground was a multipurpose megastructure containing all the householder's needs, such as shops and a post office. The town councillors, who had visited Le Corbusier's Unité d'Habitation in Marseilles in 1947, were convinced.

Once the worst slums had been identified and marked for redevelopment by the City of Glasgow in the 1950s, the run-down tenements of the Gorbals were demolished to make way for new high-rise blocks.

Through the necklace of CDA demolition was to be threaded nothing less than a full-scale motorway, the Glasgow Inner Ring Road. The scheme was reminiscent of the Bruce plan, but it had been scaled up in the manner of contemporary US cities, which a City Planning deputation had visited in 1961. The road resembled an American 'parkway', loosened up to create a swathe of free-flowing greenery in, and through, the city. The objective of the designers was

Opposite: The logical conclusion of Glasgow's Modernist-inspired approach to solving the 1960s housing crisis, the massive towers of the Red Road flats, designed by Sam Bunton, dominate their surroundings.

to create a 'linear park' in the dense grid of Central Glasgow. The north and west flanks were begun in 1965, including a high-level Clyde crossing, the Kingston Bridge, which is today buckling under the weight of gridlocked juggernauts.

Glasgow's mid-1960s combination of area redevelopment, new tower blocks and road schemes seemed to promise a slick realisation in Scotland of Modernist urbanism, presaged in improbable futurist fantasies of the 1920s. The climax of this campaign was quite awesome: a colossal group of steel-framed tower and slab blocks designed by Sam Bunton and built by the City's direct labour at Red Road, Balornock (1962–69). Many blocks were also designed as 'package deals' by contractors: for instance, Crudens's ten solemn twenty-storey slab blocks at Sighthill (1963–69). In the process, 'architecture' in the traditional sense was pushed aside. Sir Robert Matthew was sacked for demanding 'comprehensive' development of an entire area rather than opportunistic infill. Despite the astonishing success of Glasgow's schemes in terms of providing sheer numbers of new houses, many designers – having been frozen out of the process – began to say that these high blocks were not properly 'Modern' at all. Isi Metzstein declared – echoing Ruskin – that a distinction now had to be made "between architecture and building". Others argued that the problem was too urgent: people wanted homes not architecture.

During the 1960s and early 1970s, Glasgow lost nearly 200,000 inhabitants, many of them to New Towns like Cumbernauld (right). While some offered a well-planned housing mix that worked as new communities, local needs were not always best served by later schemes.

Glasgow's rehousers were serious about what they did. They believed in Glasgow and set about rebuilding its worst slums with modern houses, set in open landscaped areas to maximise the beneficial effects of space and light. Politicians, served by business, not business served by politicians, marshalled the effort. For all the well-publicised 'failure' of 1960s planning, the experience of the 1970s and 80s urban planning vacuum (planarchy?) has shown that our cities are far too precious to be left to speculators alone.

The flight to the suburbs

Between 1961 and 1975 Glasgow's population fell from over a million to 825,688, despite huge efforts made by the City. The East End was worst hit: 70% of its population was moved out. Many were lost to the New Towns of East Kilbride, Cumbernauld, Glenrothes and Irvine, but others moved just over the boundary, to new homes built by local companies. Ironically, these speculative developments of the 1960s, whether built within the boundaries or beyond, contained their own city-orientated logic. They were developed under a strict planning regime and often reflected the planners' interest in 'mixed development' of low and multi-storey housing. It was only from the later 1970s that speculative development seemed to go out of control, building according to pre-set formulas rather than local requirements.

The only effective way to bring the mushrooming suburbs back into a right relationship with the city is to plan these areas as part of the matrix of the city. In 'new communities' beyond the suburbs, we can also look to our recent history and learn from the Scottish new towns' urbanist framework, which gave places like Cumbernauld a planned coherence.

Although Glasgow has 'lost' a significant part of its rate paying or community charge-paying population, the city has not been deserted as a centre for business and entertainment. The number of tourists –

Considered urban planning was vital in areas like the Gorbals, where much of the housing stock had been rebuilt twice in one generation. As part of the larger Crown Street project, Page & Park's 1994 masterplan included Moffat Gardens by Elder & Cannon, a more open development with buildings by different architects.

including non-Glasgow residents – visiting Glasgow has grown astronomically, fuelling the city's culture-led revival. But cities need citizens: people to keep a social and cultural infrastructure alive. And it is within this context that the overall aim of the Homes for the Future has been conceived. The idea is to bring people back to live within the boundaries, to continue the regeneration of Glasgow. Developers, architects, and public bodies were asked to work together to demonstrate how exciting but affordable housing could be built in the heart of the city.

The emergence of regeneration and revival

The birth of city regeneration as we now understand the term – as sensitive rebuilding rather than comprehensive redevelopment – can be pinpointed in Scotland to 1976. The seventh New Town, Stonehouse, which would have taken yet more of Glasgow's people, was suddenly cancelled and its resources directed into 'GEAR' (Glasgow Eastern Area Renewal). The Homes for the Future site falls within this area. The city, above all else, was now seen as the appropriate arena for action: not 'clearance' but 'regeneration', driven by nostalgia for pre-clearance community life. The building type which seemed to embody this pre-Modern golden age, was the tenement, which had previously been the main target of housing reformers. Now the Modernist development replaced the tenement as the 'bad' building: 'inhuman' in scale and imposed from above. The worsening image of the private car also enabled urban motorways to be condemned out of hand – even as car ownership increased as predicted.

Ken MacRae's curved Tenement for the 21st Century, completed in 1984.

The GEAR project poured huge resources into the refurbishment and improvement of tenements following successful experiments in rehabilitation in other parts of the city. A project encouraged by GEAR in 1979 also introduced a very early Homes for the Future-type of exercise to Glasgow's East End. This was a scheme by a private firm, Unit Construction, at Dalveen Street, Shettleston. Begun in 1979, it was the first speculative housing built in the East End for 50 years. Similar projects were carried out by the developers Barratt Homes at Whiteinch and near the Homes for the Future site at Monteith Row. But it was at first assumed that owner-occupiers coming 'back' to the city from the suburbs would want a suburban-style 'cottage' dwelling. Barratt's tested the water at a site near Charing Cross in 1983–5 with a huge neo-tenement design, which was an immediate success. Clearly, they had tapped into a tenement revival.

It was in the hugely expanding area of the housing associations that architectural innovations were made. The housing associations were dubbed the 'Medici of Maryhill' by Charles McKean when they commissioned Ken MacRae's (McGurn Logan and Duncan) wonderful curved Tenement for the 21st Century at Stratford Street (1984). In parallel, there was a shift away from regeneration to 'city as monument' concerns to stop laissez-faire suburbanisation in the face of 'Brookside'-type developments of brick housing. Elder & Cannon's Duke Street block (1992), with its Alexander Thomson-esque 'attic', had split-level sections, with a severe front facade and a complex rear elevation: it was also built of beige brick laid in patterns in deference to the scale of channelled ashlar (large square-cut stones).

These earlier blocks were essentially about in-fill, but by the early 1990s, there was an increasing demand for overall 'planning'. Here, the Crown Street Project was pre-eminent. In the heart of the Gorbals where much of the housing had been swept away twice in a generation, the plan was to recreate the lost sense of urban form. The idea was inspired by the Berlin IBA, which, significantly, was an attempt to re-establish the 'Prussian block' as the basic model of future regeneration planning. The Crown Street project, masterplanned by architect Piers Gough of CZWG and run by former Glasgow city planner Mike Galloway, attempted to combine tenements and streetgrids with some privatised living space. It almost seemed that by recreating the 'image' of the tenement, its 'community spirit' could be rekindled.

At the root of the project was a strong anti-Modernist tendency but although Crown Street's first buildings were influenced by current ideas of the 'urban village', more 'open' designs were soon proposed in Gorbals East. A masterplan by Page & Park (1994) mixed a range of unified designs with Moffat Gardens at its centre. This 'garden square development' incorporated a 'dialogue' between designs by Page & Park, Simister Monaghan, and a group by Elder & Cannon with elegant twin towers. At last, the neo-tenement with its solid wall enclosing generous areas of private space had been challenged. The way was clear for a proper reassessment of 'open' modern planning.

Rear elevation of the Duke Street block by Elder & Cannon, 1992. The preceding years had seen a revival of the tenement, with speculative housing being built in Glasgow's east for the first time in 50 years and housing associations emerging as the new patrons of architecture.

Building Homes for the Future

With building on other sites due to continue until 2005, Homes for the Future is just the first phase of a regeneration project that lies at the heart of Glasgow 1999.

"The future prospect for our cities depends upon making them more desirable places to live."
Lord Rogers, from *Urban Task Force, The Task Ahead,* July 1998

The idea

In 1995, Glasgow won the right to stage a year-long cultural event: to own the coveted title of UK City of Architecture and Design, 1999. The idea for a demonstration housing project to celebrate Glasgow's reign was not part of the original bid but came from Glasgow 1999's newly-appointed director, Deyan Sudjic. Inspired by Stuttgart, Sudjic wanted to see internationally-renowned architects create signature buildings for Glasgow as part of the festival. The main objective was to "reinforce Glasgow's image as a world-class city, by providing a flagship event". But the idea went further. Glasgow's pioneering experiments in housing were to be taken to a higher level, "setting new standards of participation". All the local regeneration, housing and planning agencies would be involved – but private developers would take the lead.

Having achieved support from the Glasgow Development Agency, the City Council and the main potential funder of the project, Scottish Homes, the 'Core Group' led by Glasgow 1999 set about identifying a site. At first, the preferred location was Gorbals, where so much regeneration had already taken place. News of the scheme quickly filtered out. As one of the first big ideas to come out of Glasgow 1999 to involve actual buildings, there was great enthusiasm but there were also reservations. Some felt that Glasgow 1999 should be celebrating the city's indigenous architecture, not simply importing big names. Comparisons were made with Glasgow's year as City of Culture in 1990 when diverse international stars, from the Bolshoi Ballet to Pavarotti, were paraded before an amazed Glasgow public. Surely architecture was different? Glasgow's architects felt that they should play a part in any new-build demonstration.

A compromise was soon reached which responded to local opinion. Instead of individual dwellings, there would be a mixture – Weissenhof-style – of tenements, row houses and villas. Developers would work closely with architects on an inner city site. Insisting on teams of designers – to include one local, one UK and one world practitioner – would retain an international element in the scheme. A further issue was taken on board. Raymond Young, the driving force behind Glasgow's earlier movement for rehousing through 'rehabilitation' of tenements had devised a strategy for producing exciting, innovative architecture in social housing. This was 'SHOT' (Scotland's Homes of Tomorrow), which had the support of the key agency, Scottish Homes. So an already complex idea was further enriched as the architectural, social and economic agenda widened.

In the early stages, the project was taken forward by Vincent Wang with the assistance of project consultants Rock DCM, who began the process of identifying the site and getting the masterplan competition underway. In September 1996, management of Homes for the Future was taken over by Eleanor McAllister. The project set out to demonstrate that new and exciting architecture could play its part in stimulating the repopulation of Glasgow's East End, as well as delivering a range of exciting new houses on the edge of the historic Glasgow Green. As McAllister put it: "The exhibition shows how anyone who works in the city can live in the city. The idea is to tempt people back, but also to enrich Glasgow by building 100 homes for rent and for sale, which will combine innovative architecture with urban renewal."

The Homes for the Future site

The site chosen consists of a piece of classic brownfield land. It had been used and re-used intensively from the 1770s. Back then, it was a piece of grazing land on the edge of the growing city. It represented a development opportunity for upmarket housing, an 18th-century 'escape' from the medieval city. Much of the immediate area was laid out as a garden for David Dale's palatial house on Charlotte Street. The industrialist Dale had the grandest of a stately row of linked villas, which stood in isolation from the city until the 1820s.

Glasgow's growing prosperity was by now based on cotton, which brought wealth to managers as well as mill owners. This new class needed the lawyers, doctors, and teachers associated with a rising bourgeoisie. Their homes were centred on the River Clyde, at Carlton Place and on the North side of the river at Glasgow Green. The wealthiest had individual villas or town houses, but most were housed in upmarket tenements of a type being put up in

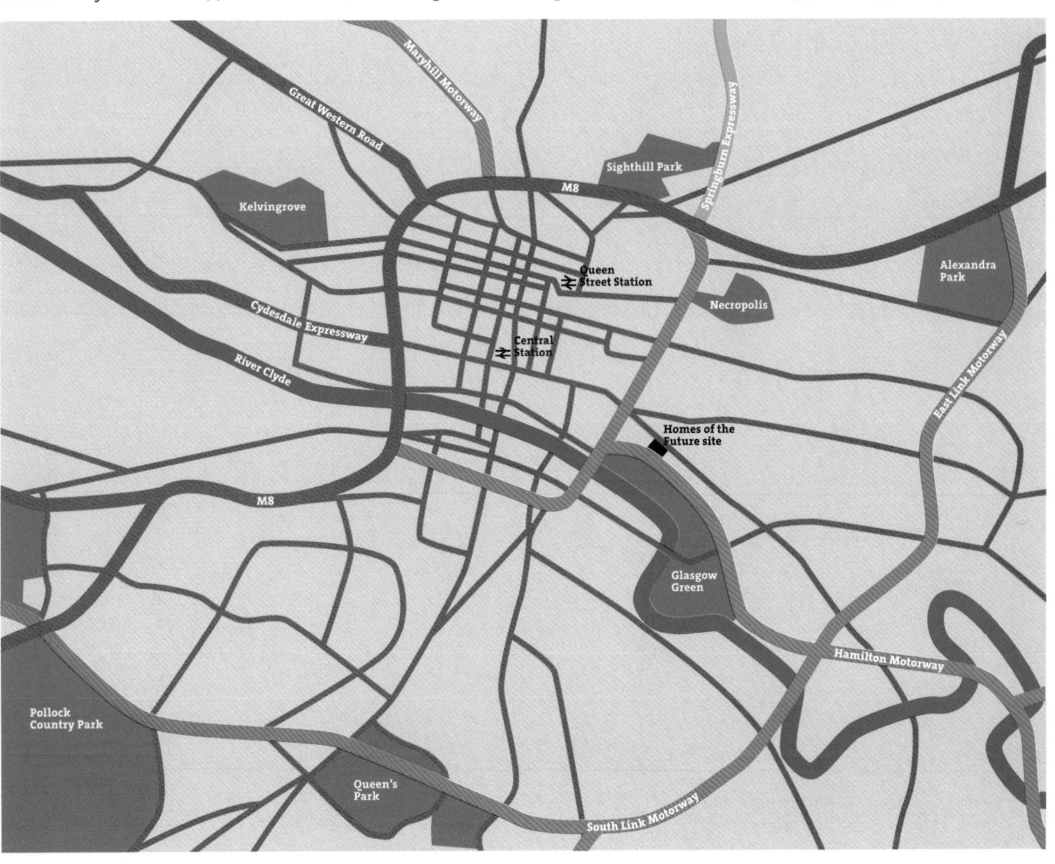

Inspired by the urban motorway networks of US cities, Glasgow's city planners set the route for the Glasgow Inner Ring Road in the early 1960s. While the north and west flanks were started in 1965 (including the Kingston Bridge over the Clyde and what is now the M8), the projected north-south link to the east of the city was never completed. Any other development plans in the subsequently blighted area around Glasgow Green were curtailed by the prospect of massive road construction.

Key

- **Existing roads**
- **Proposed motorways**
- **Expressway originally proposed as motorway**
- **River**
- **Parkland**

Edinburgh during the same period. A new 'boulevard', London Road, was driven through from Glasgow Cross to the select terrace of Monteith Row. Unemployed weavers improved the park and created a new 'avenue' at Greendyke Street. Glasgow Green became the city's playground, but also the place for often massive political demonstrations. The Green became an official public park in 1857, but large-scale industry soon made its presence felt around its edge. The Greenhead Works built gigantic steam hammers for export, and Templeton's carpet factory, a 'Camp' Coffee factory, and the noxious Hide, Skin and Tallow works all converged on the area. And as industry moved in, the middle classes moved out – to the 'caller' (fresh) air of the West End. The official endorsement of Glasgow's move west came in the 1850s with municipal involvement in the creation of an exclusive housing development grouped around a park at Woodlands Hill. However, the change in the area's fortunes was not sudden. It took place slowly but surely over the next century. From the 1950s, with the loss of industry, the whole of the East End went into accelerating decline. Finally, the area around the site was blighted by the planned north-south link of Glasgow Inner Ring Road, which was routed through Glasgow Green. Although the road was never built, it hampered any other development.

In its post-industrial condition, Glasgow has suffered more than most cities from a sterilising mixture of economic stagnation, planning blight and awkward landholdings, which combine to make creative redevelopment difficult. In the post-war period, local authorities possessed sweeping powers to deal with slum clearance and area development, but this is no longer the case. 'Regeneration' is now positively conceived as a piecemeal process, but under certain conditions of dereliction and blight, it seems that wider powers may be required. Area planning – or masterplanning as it is now called – is back on the agenda.

From the mid-19th century, Glasgow expanded rapidly, spreading west from the 1920s onwards as people left the increasingly industrial and declining east of the city.

The growth of Glasgow

- **City in 1800**
- **1846**
- **1900**
- **1925**
- **1938**
- **1975**
- **part of new S. Lanarkshire Council area (1996)**

The Homes for the Future site includes three main pieces of land, referred to as A, B and C. These are: the exhibition site (excluding the as yet undeveloped site (A4) fronting London Road); an island site to the east; and an L-shaped site on London Road and Monteith Row. Rock DCM researched the site's history and the pattern of existing infrastructure and utilities. Now the design phase of the Homes for the Future process could begin. There were two initial stages: the appointment by invited competition of a masterplanner, and then a further open competition for the design of the individual buildings. The masterplanner's role was to establish the overall vision for the site, including the size, placing and type of buildings, along with the green spaces. The three invited entrants were Bonar and Grams with Shane O'Toole, McKeown Alexander with Teun Koolhaas, and Page & Park with Ove Arup Associates. Bonar and Grams/Shane O'Toole proposed a bold series of towers set on a continuous service and commercial podium. "All buildings on the podium become icons," they argued. The site was to become a 'super-block' with an 'apartment tower' on London Road. The scheme demanded a very strong design lead and seemed to limit potential collaboration between architects because of the podium and tower formula. McKeown Alexander and Teun Koolhaas produced an even more striking piece of open modernity, with an 'informal park' penetrating the buildings. In their plan, geometrically-placed towers marched into the Green, whose space also flowed back between the structures to create a "juxtaposition of buildings and open space". Again, there was little scope for heterogeneity of form. The plan needed to marshal identical blocks to achieve an effect. By contrast, the winning scheme by Page & Park proposed a gentler mixture of terrace, 'villa' and larger-scale flatted blocks, 'filling' the three sites but offering the possibility for a flexible collection of buildings set around semi-private, rather than completely open gardens.

Within the masterplan, 'development parcels' were identified, "that represent a variety of housing and mixed use opportunities". Page & Park also drew up design guidelines in consultation with Glasgow 1999. The object was to create "visual coherence and an overall sense of appropriateness". However, the masterplanners were at pains to point out that "these guidelines do not preclude the introduction of landmark or iconic buildings". The plan also specified 'landscape principles' and here again there was a wish to create a kind of neo-Modernist 'openness' with 'semi-private' parks in several of the land parcels. There was also guidance as to permitted densities: site A2, for example, facing the Green with apartment buildings (buildings nine, ten, and one) had a notional 34 units on 2,250 square metres, whereas site A3 (the two terraces, buildings seven and eight) would have 20 units on 2,850 square metres. As built, site A2 has 41 units and A3 has 20 as outlined. The differential illustrates the flexibility of the tenement (or apartment block) over the town house.

It was the introduction of 'landmark' buildings along with the openness of the plan which seemed to irk celebrated Glasgow architect Isi Metzstein. Metzstein has argued that the scheme's flamboyant buildings did not respect Glasgow's "urban grain". The whole scheme, he said in the *Architects' Journal*, was "an architectural zoo" of competing species. The criticism got to the heart of an issue that Glasgow has been debating ever since. This is the question of whether to rebuild the broken edges of the city's celebrated 'grid' (even where it had not previously existed) or to reassess the whole situation, allowing for new approaches to urban coherence. A decision in favour of flexibility had already been made at the masterplan stage: re-establish an 'edge' where necessary (Greendyke Street, London Road) but also offer permeability and openness where appropriate (Charlotte Street/Greendyke Street). As part of the developers' submissions, the housebuilders Miller Homes offered to take the whole site, but this was rejected by the judging panel as "too much of the same thing". Also, Miller's were reluctant to guarantee delivery of the whole site for July 1999.

The inevitable result of the collaborative nature of Homes for the Future has been heterogeneity: different approaches by different architects, all working together on one site. However Glasgow 1999 has regarded this not as a defect, but as the positive result of a dynamic collaboration.

Of course, the remaining 'cleared' areas of the East End of Glasgow could be built up again with neo-tenements, enclosing large areas of privatised space. All that would be missing would be the vast chimneys of the Parkhead Forge, on whose economic might almost the whole area was based. But to embark on a plan like that would be to romanticise the distant past and to demonise recent history with its planned open space. Such a scheme might even echo the sterility of Glasgow's 1950s peripheral tenements, without the enlivening features of churches and schools to break the monotony.

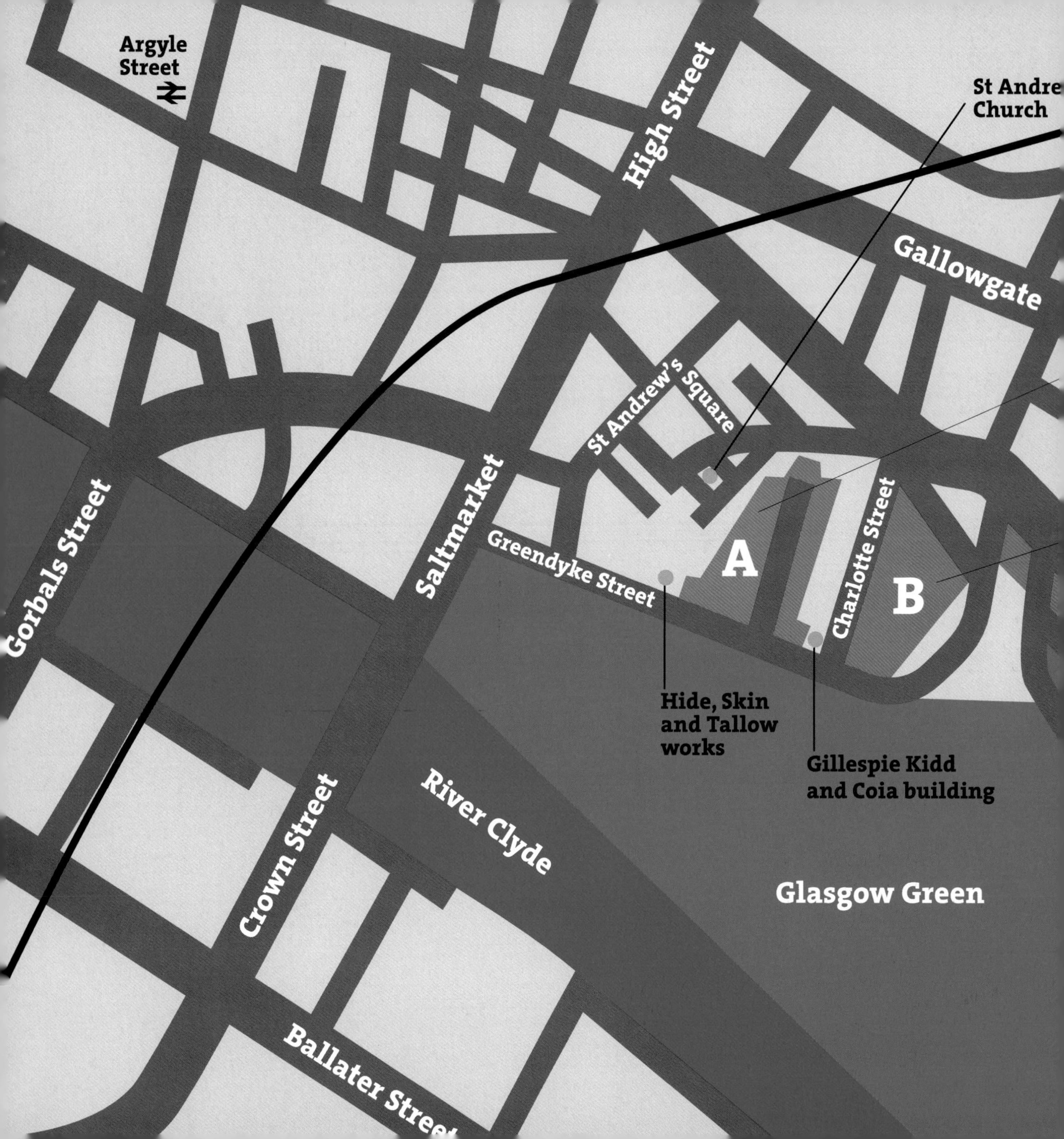
Argyle
Street
St Andre
Church
High Street
Gallowgate
St Andrew's Square
Saltmarket
Greendyke Street
Charlotte Street
A
B
Gorbals Street
Hide, Skin
and Tallow
works
Gillespie Kidd
and Coia building
River Clyde
Crown Street
Glasgow Green
Ballater Stree

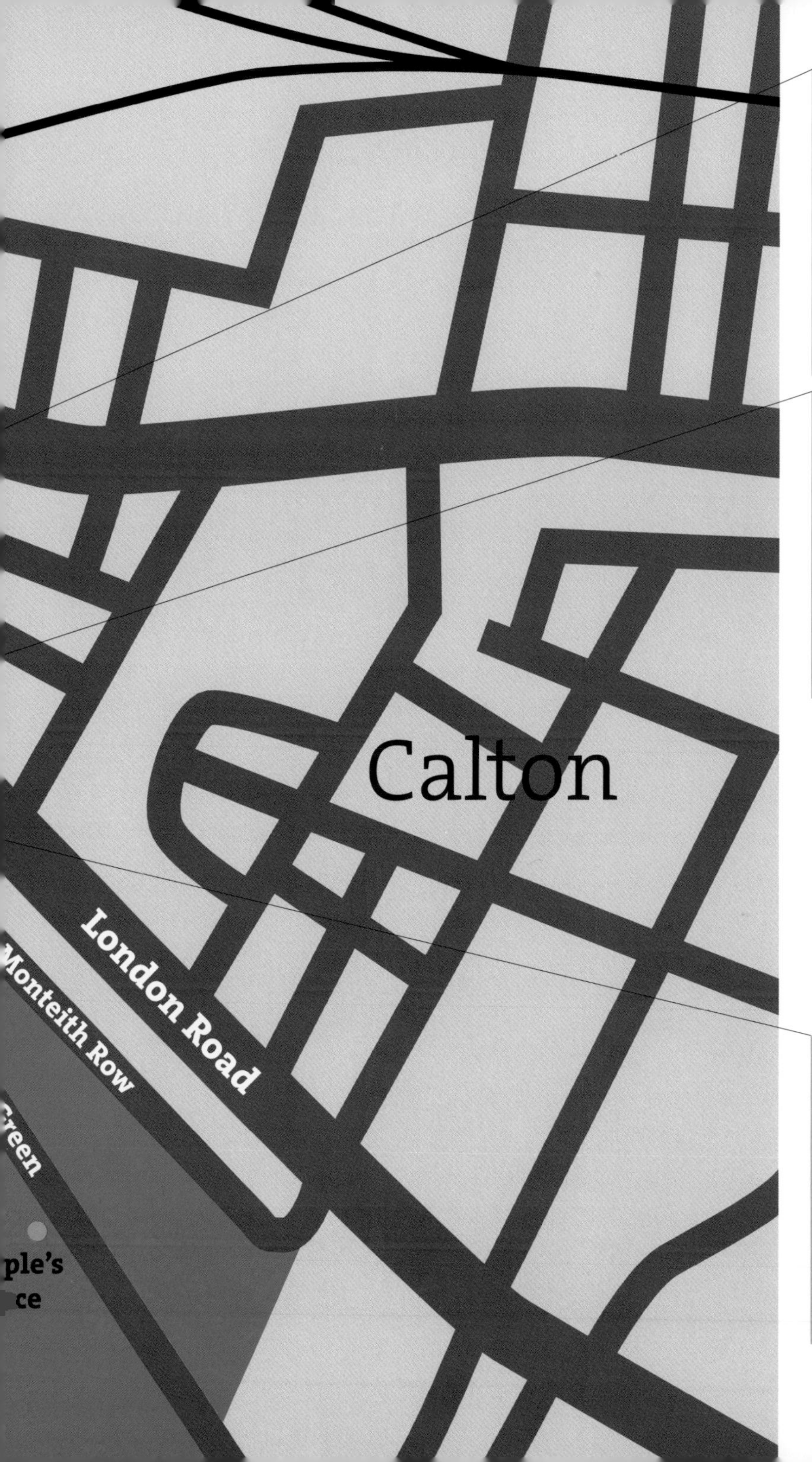

Site A: Homes for the Future

London Road, Charlotte Street, St Andrew's Square, Greendyke Street: very much a backland feel beyond the prestigious 'grand apartment' blocks of Greendyke Street. But unlike earlier schemes, instead of privatising the back area around an 'inhabited wall' of tenements, the scheme uses the different character of the rear of the site to create a more intimate public/private space fronted by smaller houses.

Site B: Homes for the Future 2

The triangular form of Site B is the most prominent of the masterplan area. The site juts into the notional parkland, acting as a hinge between the urbanity of Charlotte Street and the openness of Glasgow Green. The site can also act as a gateway to the park. The current masterplan proposes a tenement-style building to London Road, a 'point' block of seven storeys or more on the hinge and smaller scale houses in between.

Site C Homes for the Future 3

Site C has a stronger connection with site B. A 'new icon' building is planned to enclose the entrance to Glasgow Green along the setpiece avenue which was cut through the park in 1900 to give access to the People's Palace.

Prior to redevelopment, the site was a blighted wasteland. Nevertheless, it was surrounded by buildings of historical significance to the city. These include St Andrew's Church (middle right of picture); David Dale's palatial house (bottom left of picture); Gillespie, Kidd and Coia's brutalist school (top left of picture) and one of the last remaining villas facing onto Glasgow Green (top right of picture). The masterplan had to ensure that these existing structures were not overpowered. Opposite: Page & Park's winning masterplan allowed for a variety of different building types.

The process

After the site was chosen, Glasgow 1999 staged two competitions: one to select a masterplanner, the second to choose the developers and their architects.

In the scheme submitted by Miller Homes, two connected buildings by Van Berkel & Bos frame communal gardens. The low cedar-clad 'town house' blocks were located behind three taller blocks facing Glasgow Green by David Chipperfield Associates and Holmes Partnership.

The developers' submissions

Working within the terms of the masterplan for a mixed development, developers were asked to team up with architects to provide a range of house types for the site. Three architects were to be involved in each submission: one from Glasgow, a British architect, and an international designer. Entries were received from Miller Homes with the Holmes Partnership, Van Berkel and Bos and David Chipperfield Architects; from John Dickie with Elder and Cannon, Rick Mather Architects, and Odile Decq and Benoit Cornette; from The Burrell Company with McKeown Alexander Architects, Richard Murphy Architects and Ushida Findlay; and from Logan Construction with RMJM, Craiglinn with Coleman Ballantine and Simister Monaghan. From a complicated mix, the judging panel chose two main developers, Dickie and Burrell.

After the judging panel had made its choice of developers, a complex situation arose. The job of masterplanners and project managers Rock DCM was to put together a scheme that would provide mixed housing in a dynamic, creative and realistic package. A second stage of developers' submissions then took place. Five developers and seven architects were mixed and matched, to the dismay of some such as Richard Murphy and Odile Decq/Benoit Cornette who lost out. Bonar Grams/Shane O'Toole lost out twice, at both the masterplan and the design stage, with their superb "domestic hi-fi object in an urban scale" for Greendyke Street submitted by Logan Construction. The developers Mactaggart and Mickel with Wren Rutherford joined Dickie and Burrell and Logan Construction with RMJM replacing the earlier appointees, Craiglinn, who had worked up an interesting, extravagantly-roofed terrace for Site A5c with Vernon Monaghan and Coleman Ballantine.

A development agreement was drawn up by Rock DCM and agreed by all parties. In only six weeks planning permission was obtained and the work

Odile Decq and Benoit Cornette explored the possibility of creating a landmark structure facing Glasgow Green, marking the entrance to the inner courtyard at the heart of the scheme. In the end, the site was allocated to the Ushida Findlay building.

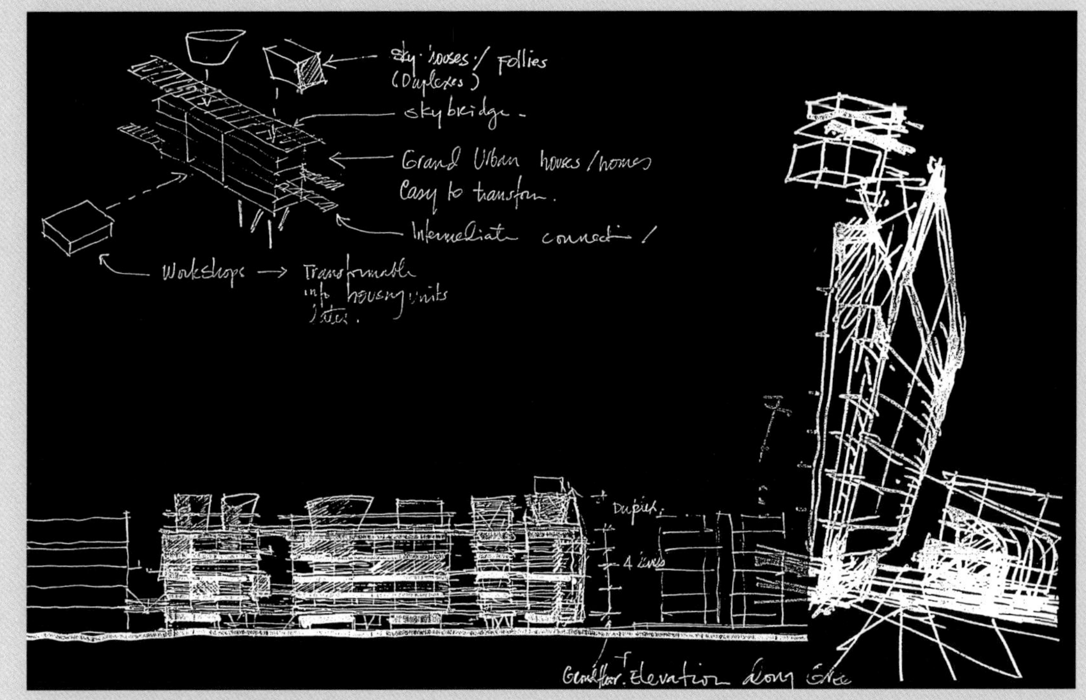

"In the wider context, Homes for the Future has something important to contribute, regardless of whether the scheme is ultimately groundbreaking or not. You get used to seeing modern housing in places like Paris, but we've been denied that chance over here. Maybe this project can open up opportunities for discussion by giving people a new talking point, right on their doorstep." *Ian Alexander, McKeown Alexander*

began. The key to this astonishing turnaround time was the Core Group, whose individual planners, roads engineers and funding bodies had already been fully involved with the process, contributing to a groundbreaking 'planning day' held in April 1998. Fast-track construction strategies were used and a limited mix of external materials – white render, red cedar and steel – was agreed in order to achieve cohesion without uniformity. Only one building, Ian Ritchie's block for Thenew, sets itself apart with its brilliant use of copper cladding.

Public funding

Scottish Homes awarded grant aid to developers for units with a value of £60,000 or under. Grant aid was also awarded to Thenew Housing association for social rented housing. 45 out of a total of 99 units have had grant assistance for low-cost home ownership and 12 units for social rented housing. In a groundbreaking move, a small number of 'lofts' (shell apartments to be fitted out later to the owner's specification) have been targeted at the lower end of

Two very different approaches: Chipperfield, Holmes and van Berkel & Bos, working for Miller Homes, would have produced the rigorous geometry of the scheme below, while Decq and Cornette, part of the team organised by Elder &Cannon, would have been more flamboyant (right).

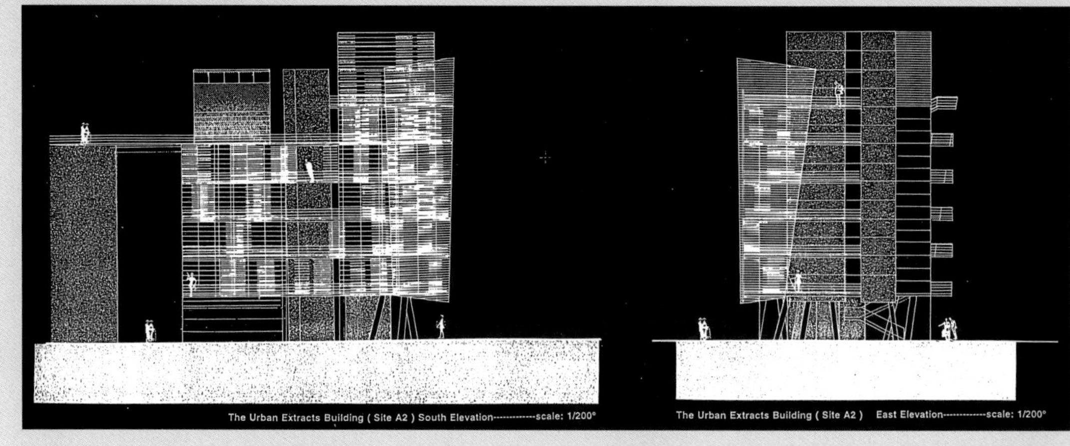

"It's a miracle that we built Homes for the Future in only eight months, but what this project has to say is more important than how it was constructed. It shows that intensity of development can be combined with the variety and creativity needed to reflect our changing society. John Richards, a founding partner of RMJM, described the scheme as being like a jazz band improvising – some of the collaborations worked seamlessly, others were more discordant, but all the elements add up to a harmonious whole." *David Page, Page & Park*

the home ownership market, thereby promoting flexibility as opposed to predetermined units such as 'family' or 'single person'.

What now?

Homes for the Future has been one of the most talked-about housing projects of the last ten years. It has taken Glasgow's reputation for architectural excellence in housing association work and exuberantly applied it to a mixed development of private and social rented homes. Developers have suddenly sat up and taken notice. Already there is a huge amount of interest in the two remaining masterplan sites and in the continuing redevelopment of nearby Gorbals. In the West End of the city there have been developer-led schemes designed by innovative architectural practices such as Cooper Cromar at Byres Road, Anderson Christie at Saltoun Street and Elder & Cannon at Cleveden Road. The message seems to be that good design will sell. Outside of Glasgow, the influence of Homes for the Future is seen in many regeneration schemes. The 'Urban Splash' competition in Manchester, for example, comes very close, particularly Arca's unsuccessful scheme which seems to echo Ian

After the competition process, elements from various developers' proposals were put together to create the agreed scheme for the first stage of the project.

"Under the umbrella of Glasgow 1999, all these different organisations pulled together to create a project that is successful both aesthetically and commercially. Homes for the Future has undoubtedly led the way in suggesting that our inner city areas should be considered more imaginatively to offer new models for living. As a direct result of this project, land values in the area have increased and regeneration is well under way." *David McAllister, Rock DCM*

Ritchie's linked twin towers. However, the developer's wish to "get away from neo-Georgian boxes" in urban regeneration also strikes a similar chord. Although it had an immensely complicated lead-in and demanded an enormous amount of hard work, Homes for the Future has nevertheless been well worth it. The project has shown that through a collaborative effort of local and national regeneration agencies, working with communities and developers, urban projects can be as attractive to developers as greenfield, suburban sites.

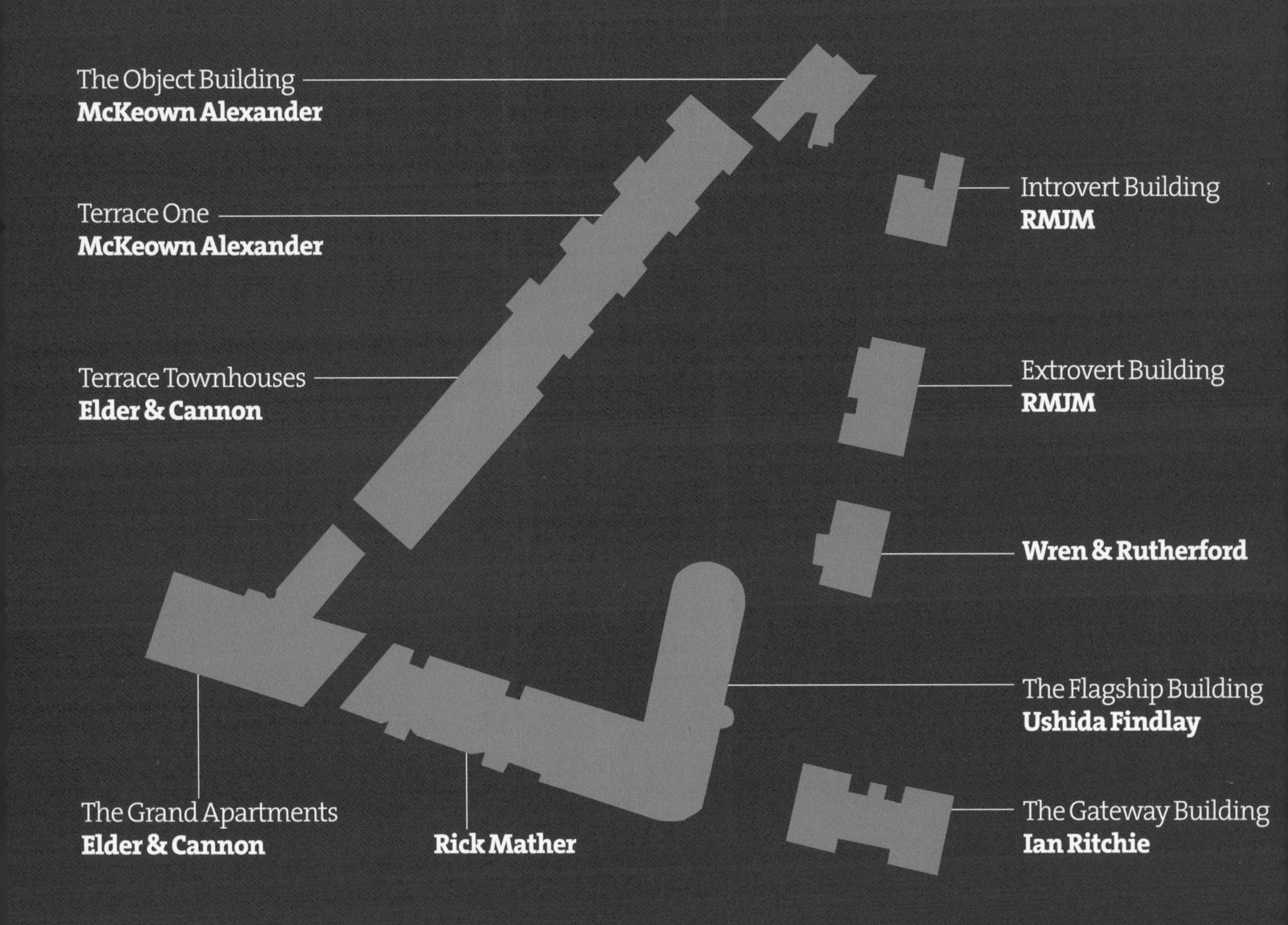

Homes for the Future

Naomi Stungo describes the projects completed in the first phase of the project, and meets the architects responsible for each building.

HOMES FOR THE FUTURE
HOMES FOR THE

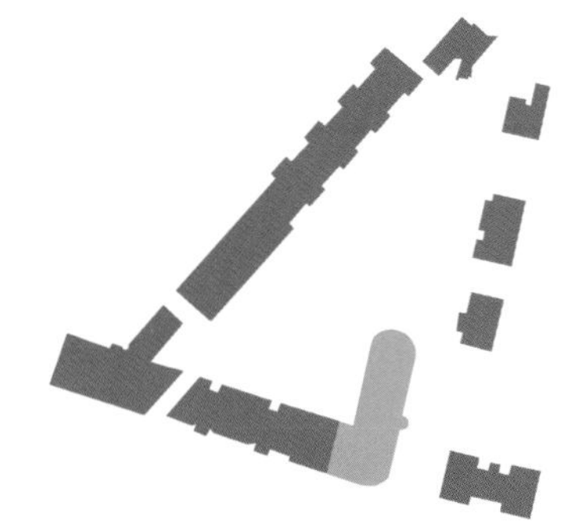

The Glasgow Green project is the first chance that Tokyo-based architects Ushida Findlay have had to build in Europe. Their block defines an important corner on the site, then cascades down in a series of terraces.

Ushida Findlay

this way

It was with a trio of astonishing houses – the Echo Chamber House, the Truss Wall House and the Soft and Hairy House – that the Tokyo-based Ushida Findlay Partnership burst onto the architectural scene in the early 1990s. Architects worldwide were dazzled by the houses' strange moulded forms, their mixing of architecture and landscape, and their sheer audacity.

"Our approach to architecture," explains Kathryn Findlay, "is to create inclusive space. It's a hybrid of disciplines – primarily architecture and landscape. We don't stick to one solution: we are chameleon-like, our reference point is chaos-based geometry."

Scottish-born Findlay and her husband, Tokyo-raised Eisaku Ushida, met in Japan in the early 1980s while both were working in the offices of Arata Isozaki, one of the country's leading architects. For Findlay it was her first job after studying at London's Architectural Association; Ushida had previously worked in the Richard Rogers Partnership's London offices. Finding in each other, despite their cultural differences, an enormous overlap in interests, the pair set up in partnership together in 1986.

Today their architecture spans continents – they have offices in Tokyo and London – and disciplines: as well as practising, both teach (she is the first woman assistant professor at Tokyo University, he is visiting professor at UCLA in the US). What unites everything they do, however, is a desire to push ideas to the limit, says their London-based associate John Nordon.

This determination to stretch and test ideas can be seen even in their earliest projects. The Truss Wall House used an innovative form of concrete construction (in which sections are formed from bent steel reinforcing bars that are welded together and overlaid with a fine wire mesh, over which concrete is poured) to create an astonishing moulded form more reminiscent of a giant piece of hi-fi or sports equipment than it is of a house. The Soft and Hairy House is similarly unconventional: a loosely-organised courtyard house at whose centre is a free-standing pod – the bathroom which, like a Turkish bath, is perforated with glass discs which bring daylight into otherwise dark space. A jungle of planting on the building's flat roof adds a soft, 'hairy' finish to the whole assembly.

Although the partnership has now built several houses, been shortlisted for a number of prestigious competitions and won awards, Homes for the Future is Ushida Findlay's biggest job by a long way. Its design, though, is clearly descended from some of the practice's earlier projects. Findlay describes their terraced block of apartments as a "comfortable body glove" and, with its curving form fronting the street and cascading stepped terraces of planting at the rear, there is definitely something organic about the scheme.

Whether the practice will now break into the British scene remains to be seen. It is a promising sign that the London office, set up in 1997, already has more staff than Tokyo (although this doesn't take account of Findlay's students' contribution to the practice) and that it has been quick to pick up jobs. Ushida Findlay is definitely a practice to watch.

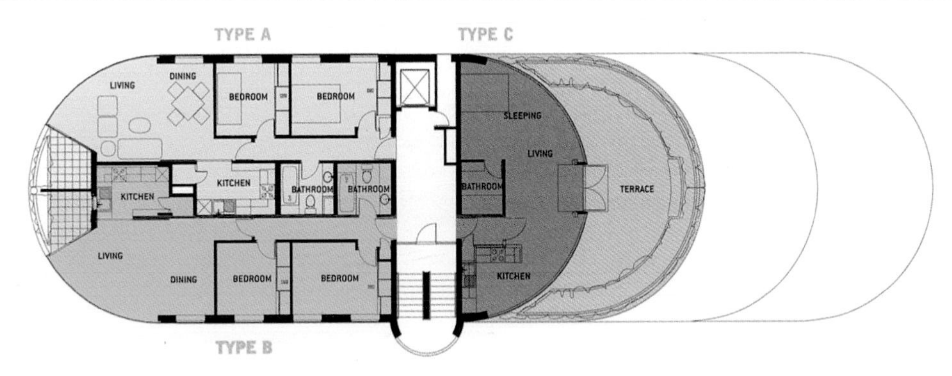

Ushida Findlay subdivide each floor to offer a variety of flats, but each of them has the possibility of a balcony overlooking Glasgow Green, or a garden terrace at the rear.

The stepped tail of the block bridges over an opening that allows access to the internal courtyard and its car park. Opposite: balconies face south toward Glasgow Green.

One of three buildings constructed by the Burrell Company on the Homes for the Future site, the Flagship Building consists of eight loft-style apartments, as well as a penthouse, two three-bedroom flats, a two-bedroom flat, and a one-bedroom flat. It also has space for a commercial unit on the ground floor. "Our building is designed to blur the boundary between living inside and living outside," claim the architects, Ushida Findlay. "It is wrapped in glass to allow enjoyment of the surrounding views, steps its terraces down to the garden and drapes itself in planting."

The result is a building of stepped terraces which reach progressively further out into the courtyard towards the base of the structure. It also fulfills the brief of the Burrell Company, who were looking for "a building that would address the vehicular entrance to the site but respond to the inner courtyard, thus the commercial units, some larger apartments, lofts and terraces".

Constructed from concrete floor slabs cast on columns in situ, with a steel-frame mezzanine and penthouse, the Flagship Building is clad with double glazing, with a variety of fittings, aluminium framing and elsewhere with insulated rendered panels. On a pergola-style frame which descends the terraces like a ski-jump, plants will be grown, emphasising and softening the terracing, while also presenting a sympathetic view from the courtyard.

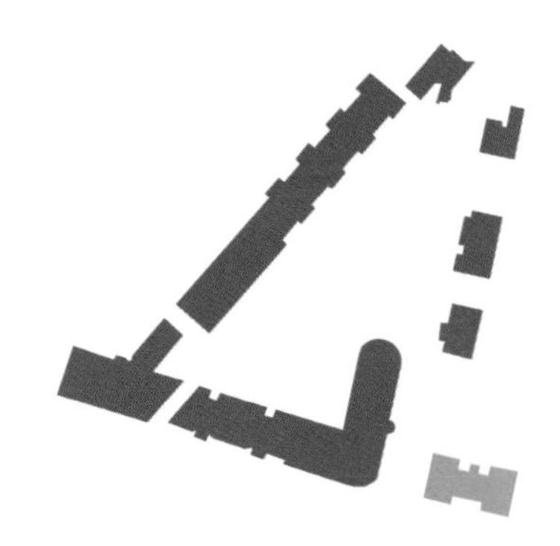

Ian Ritchie

Ian Ritchie won a competition run by the Thenew Housing Association to design this block which adjoins Isi Metzstein's listed former school building on the edge of the Homes for the Future site. The apartments in this copper-clad building will be rented to housing association tenants.

Apartments are in two groups, on either side of the recessed core in which stairs and lift are accommodated. Maximum flexibility in internal planning is allowed by the steel structure.

"Our conceptual thinking," explains Ian Ritchie, "integrates art, science, technology, economy with architecture and landscape."

Of the seven practices designing Glasgow's Homes for the Future, Ian Ritchie Architects is possibly the most multi-disciplinary in its approach. It is typical of Ritchie's breadth of interests that in 1981, the same year he set up Ian Ritchie Architects, he also helped found Rice Francis Ritchie, a loose collaboration between the brilliant structural engineer Peter Rice, the industrial designer and naval architect Martin Francis, and Ritchie. The Paris-based company was responsible for, among other projects, the 'cloud' that hangs under the arch at La Defence and the bioclimatic facades at La Villette.

The work done by Ian Ritchie Architects is just as broad-based. Some of its projects are at the cutting edge of research and development – creating light-transmitting fabrics with European aeronautics companies, or coatings for glass that have a 'memory' built in. But it is not all hi-tech gizmos: the practice is just as interested in old-fashioned institutions such as museums – it created dramatic new glass lifts for the Reina Sofia Museum of modern art in Madrid; as it is in housing and infrastructure – it designed the new Jubilee Line station at Bermondsey.

For Ian Ritchie, architecture is about creating buildings that work both on an urban and a social level. "We must strive," he explains, "to make urban living more attractive at every level... If, as I believe, much of our city environment can be described as visually poor, it is important to ask what message this aesthetic poverty communicates to the general public. I suggest it conveys a lack of morality; hurts the viewer's sensibilities and, in so doing, becomes a symbol of harm. It has the effect of slowly wearing you down. There is a general lowering of aspiration and expectation. People are numbed to the extent that they accept or, more dangerously, ignore the low quality of their surroundings."

Urban planning has always been one of the practice's strong points. In addition to work in this country – such as masterplans for London's White City and Docklands areas and a regeneration strategy for Digbeth in Birmingham – it has won commissions to create development plans for areas in Finland and France.

Its scheme for Homes for the Future unites these various themes. The Glasgow 1999 project as a whole ties into the practice's concern for creating dense, sustainable urban environments. Its particular contribution – a set-back stand alone block – defers to its context and the (grade I) listed Gillespie Kidd and Coia school adjacent to the site, and yet it is bold and modern too. Designed as a prototype for urban living, it grows out of the practice's interest in research and development, while working with artist Jane Kelly ties in to its arts experience. It is exactly the sort of multi-disciplinary approach you would expect from such a multi-disciplinary practice.

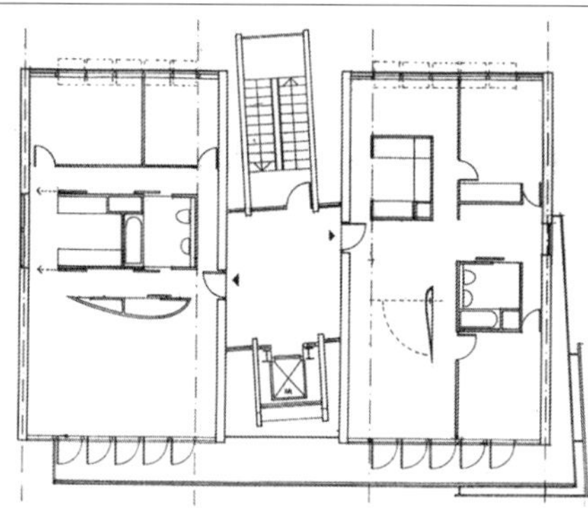

Thenew Housing Association commissioned Ian Ritchie to design the Gateway Building on the eastern edge of the Homes for the Future site, and in a sensitive location next to an important example of modernist architecture designed in the 1960s by Isi Metzstein of Gillespie, Kidd and Coia. Thenew's aim was to create "flexible, barrier-free, affordable rented homes for city centre living, marrying innovative design with energy efficiency, good sound insulation and air quality."

In response to this brief, Ian Ritchie has designed the six-storey Gateway Building which contains twelve identically-sized two bedroom flats. The building's height, say the architects, "continues the urban scale, edging Glasgow Green and developed spatially from the idea of outdoor rooms which separate each apartment."

These 'outdoor rooms' are articulated as units set back from the dramatic copper-clad façade of the building, and allow a view of the tensioned steel frame on which the copper is hung.

Unfinished at the time of publication, the building is set to provide a dramatic addition to the Glasgow Green elevation of the Homes for the Future site. Inside, the apartments will be equally exuberant, utilising exposed concrete and coloured screed, as well as timber flooring.

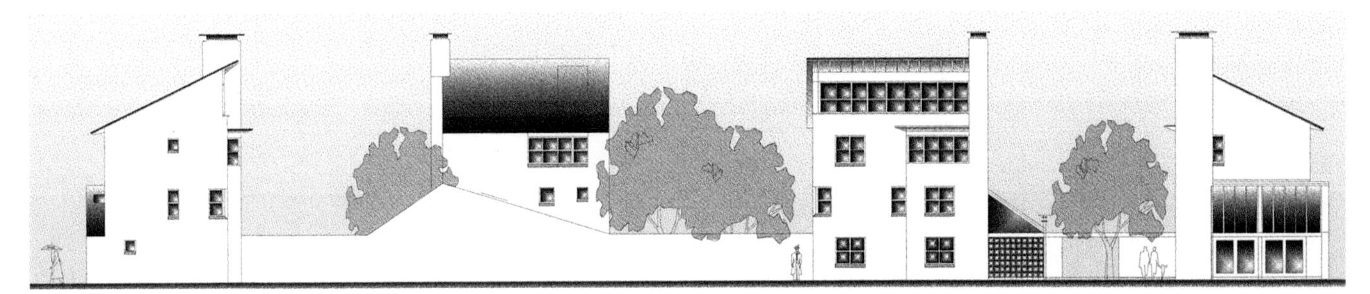

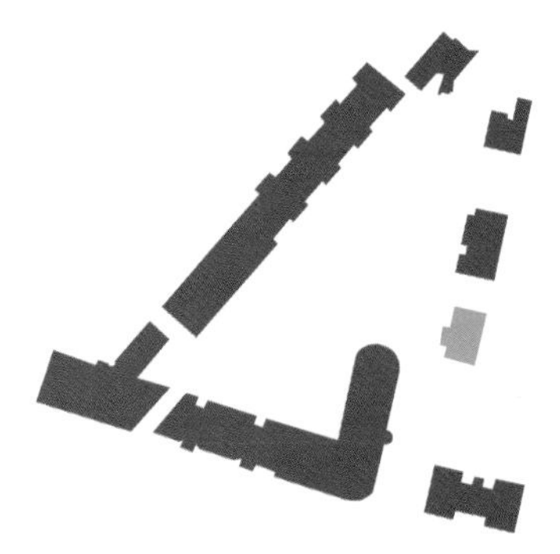

The building designed by Wren Rutherford may draw on traditional Scottish architectural forms and materials, but by considering issues such as energy efficiency and disabled access, the architects are looking towards the future of housing.

HOME

"Modern contextualism" is how Roan Rutherford characterises his practice's approach to design. "We use traditional materials in a modern style," he explains. "We are interested in working with the vernacular in a contemporary way and, since we always build in Scotland, ours is a Scottish contextualism."

This concern for Scottish heritage is deep-rooted. Rutherford and his co-director George Wren have long been part of the Scottish architectural scene. Rutherford, a prominent architect and town planner, and Wren, a past president of the Royal Incorporation of Architects in Scotland, met while working at Irvine Development Corporation. When this wound up at the end of 1996, the pair set up in practice together just a few miles down the west coast from Irvine in the southern-Scottish town of Ayr. Wren Rutherford immediately picked up the accolade of Best Architect in the Scottish Architectural Awards.

Although the practice remains small (it employs just six staff) it has quickly grown in importance. It now has offices in Glasgow and is, since 1998, part of the Austin-Smith:Lord group of architectural practices, a tie-up that links it with offices in London, Warrington and Cardiff and brings back-up administration and research assistance – although no imposed house style.

Like many small practices, Wren Rutherford ASL's workload is a complete mix. The housing work with which both directors were involved during their time at Irvine Development Corporation continues, now for private developers rather than the public sector.

In addition to housing (which also includes special needs projects) the practice has worked on industrial projects, recreational and educational buildings and fit-outs. It has also acquired a reputation for restoring listed buildings and working on historically sensitive sites. Projects, across the board, tend to be in the £250,000-£5,000,000 range.

Looking at the brochure that Wren Rutherford ASL sends out – a publication dominated by images of award-winning vernacular-style housing in conservation areas – the practice does not immediately appear an obvious choice for the Homes for the Future project. There is none of Ushida Findlay's futuristic sculptural form-making in their work, nor Ian Ritchie's interest in industrial technology. And yet, listening to Rutherford talk about their scheme, it is apparent that the practice has a very clear idea about housing for the future.

"Disability access and energy conservation are key issues for us," he explains, "Homes for the Future ought to be accessible to all, not just the able-bodied. Ours is the only project on-site to be completely wheelchair accessible. We also believe that making buildings energy efficient is the way forward."

In this respect the practice's contribution to the debate is invaluable, reminding us, as it does, that innovation is not just a formal challenge – that buildings need not necessarily look remarkable to be remarkable. Although the practice's project is the smallest of the Homes for the Future schemes and the most conventional-looking, it plays an important role in promoting a new model for living.

Wren Rutherford's building provides flexible accomodation for living and working – the triplex apartment over the self-contained barrier-free ground floor flat is designed with the needs of people working from home in mind.

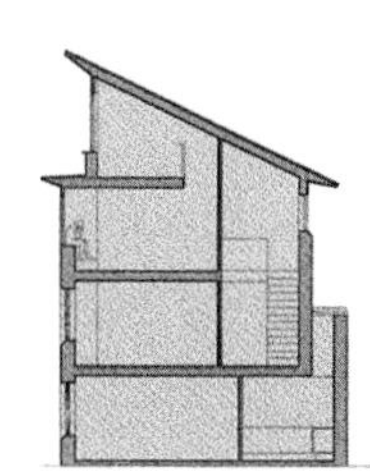
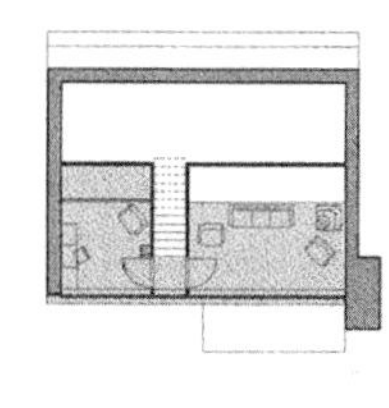
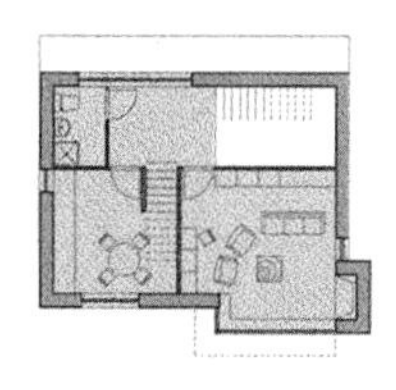
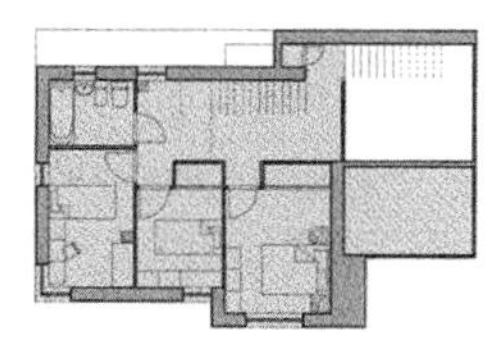
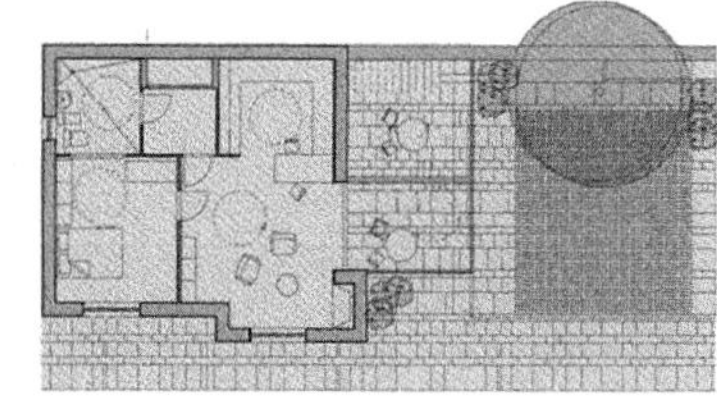

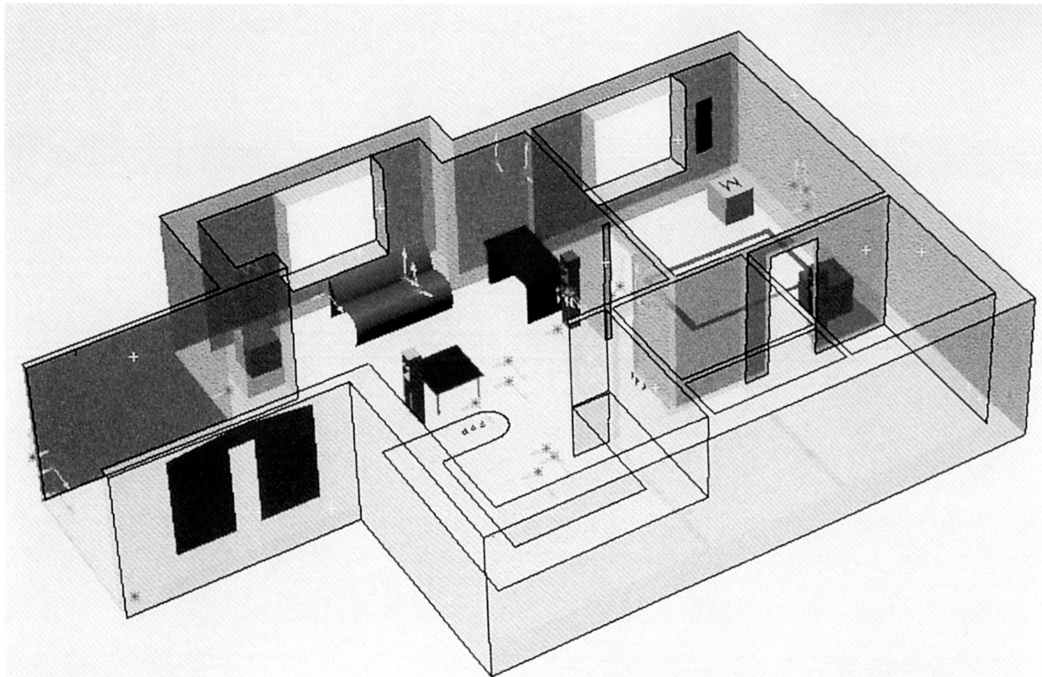

The ground floor flat (above) is designed to be completely wheelchair-accessible. As part of the 'Picture this – design that' project, Mike Anusas and James Anwyl collaborated on an installation showing new products for people with impaired sight or hearing, or restricted mobility.

Developer Mactaggart & Mickel chose to work with Wren Rutherford, with the aim of developing "an innovative design of a home for the future." The resulting building draws on Scottish vernacular architecture, but places a particular emphasis on energy conservation and access for wheelchair users. It consists of a one-bedroom flat which is barrier-free to allow freedom of access, and a two-bedroom triplex (an apartment on three levels) with flexible space to allow for contemporary home/office requirements.

"The building is designed to catch and conserve solar energy," claim the architects. "Its form is derived from the expression of the construction, using the chimney as the focal point of the composition."

The building is constructed using load-bearing blockwork walls, with timber floors (as well as a concrete separating floor between the two apartments) and a pitched roof. The exterior is covered with smooth render MR, and the roof clad with concrete roof tiles and photovoltaic (solar) roof panels.

At first sight, the timber-framed Extrovert and Introvert Buildings designed by RMJM are far removed from the classic Scottish tenement. But the adjoining blocks, with their shared staircase and emphasis on communality, are a logical development of Glasgow's favourite form of housing.

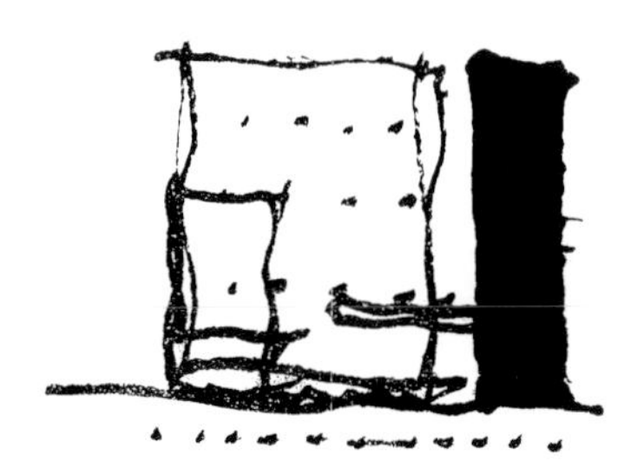

Previous pages: Tom Dixon's installation in the RMJM building, one of a number of specially-commissioned interiors created as part of the Homes for the Future Expo. Opposite: the exterior shares the vocabulary of timber board and white render used by its neighbours.

The rehabilitation of RMJM was complete when the style gurus from *Wallpaper** magazine declared the 1969 Czech Embassy in London to be not only their favourite RMJM building, but also the ideal *Wallpaper** office.

Founded over 40 years ago, RMJM (always referred to as "rum-jum") was the force behind some of the most striking architecture of the 1960s. Its New Zealand House in London's Haymarket was as stylish as its Commonwealth Institute in Kensington was bold. Still one of the larger British practices, it seemed to lose impetus during the 1980s (it is difficult to think of a single remarkable RMJM design from the period). The 1990s, however, have seen RMJM's return to form.

"What we are doing today is revisiting the practice's roots," says Paul Stallan, who set up the Glasgow office four years ago. "It is good modern work designed with humility."

The Glasgow office, with its 14-strong staff, is RMJM's newest. The practice has always had offices in both London and Edinburgh, but finally decided that a Glasgow presence was necessary to capitalise on work both in the city and along the west coast of Scotland. The move seems to have paid off: since Stallan set up in Drummond Street on the back of work at Glasgow Caledonia University, the Glasgow practice has mushroomed.

Today, the Homes for the Future project is the practice's smallest current project. In addition to the ongoing masterplan to rework Caledonia University, it has two projects at Stirling University, PFI (private finance initiative) commissions, commercial work and a continuous stream of competition entries. It has also established a tie-up with a Dubai-based practice, a collaboration which has led to a range of exotic projects including designing the new Dubai stock exchange, extending the main race course and building a gold-working facility.

What characterises the practice's approach to this diverse range of projects, Stallan says, is its engineered stand on design: "The end product is always highly influenced by structural rationalism and approaches to technology. We like to come up with rational solutions."

And yet there is a strong interest in the arts, too. One of the first projects to be completed by the Glasgow office was the redevelopment of Glasgow's Tron Theatre. There are also frequent collaborations with artists: the practice worked with Alison Turnbull on its Millennium Bridge competition entry and has teamed up with artist Robin Lee for the Homes for the Future project.

It is perhaps not surprising, then, that Stallan describes RMJM's Homes for the Future scheme as a "big Donald Judd box". The building is in keeping with a RMJM tradition of "robustness" he says, describing the building's language as "small but muscular". But it also pushes RMJM traditions. A five-storey timber frame construction – which is unusually tall for timber buildings in this country – it advances a green agenda and takes the practice into new territories as it approaches the end of the millennium.

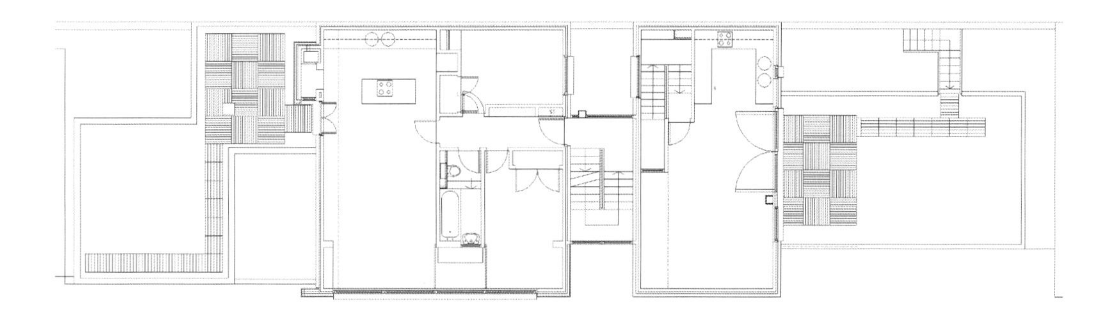

The roof of the RMJM building has been turned into an extensive landscaped garden, with spectacular views over the centre of Glasgow and the rest of the Homes for the Future development.

Designed by the Glasgow office of architecture practice RMJM for developer Logan Construction Management, the Extrovert Building consists of a one-bedroom flat, a two-bedroom flat, three flats with three bedrooms, a two-bedroom maisonette, a two/three-bedroom maisonette, and a three-bedroom maisonette. It is the larger of two adjoining buildings by RMJM on the site, and is described by the architects as "extrovert".

"The design team was encouraged to innovate and explore a new model for future living within the city. Large areas of glass on the 'extrovert' block are played off against more closed facades – the 'introvert' – arranged on either side of shared staircases," claim the architects.

Although its approach is technologically experimental, RMJM's building also draws on the traditional language of Glasgow's tenement buildings, apartments which cluster around a shared staircase to form a 'close'. For the developers, it's the ideal mix: "This is a building that explores technology: the 'tenemental close' of tomorrow".

The structure consists of a timber frame, clad with Western Red Cedar wood and Powerwall render. Detail is provided by aluminium flashings and trims, as well as galvanised mild steel handrails on the exterior staircases.

The discrete elements of the RMJM/Logan development are unified by their geometric clarity, and the consistency with which they use a restricted palette of materials.

The second of RMJM's buildings for developer Logan consists of a two-bedroom flat and a three-bedroom maisonette.

According to the architects, this building is the more 'introvert' of the two adjoining blocks, utilising an approach which is less clearly based on the communality of the tenement. It has, nevertheless, been carefully conceptualised in terms of its communality with the other buildings on the Homes for the Future site. "Both of our buildings on the site are integrated with the garden wall of the Wren Rutherford block, and by extension to the Ian Ritchie's 'Gateway' building," say the architects.

The developers, Logan Construction Management, are enthusiastic about the result. "Using an excellent professional team, we are offering an imaginative, high-quality design that seeks to change public perceptions of what can be available in social and public housing."

The Introvert Building's structure consists of a timber frame, clad with Western Red Cedar wood and Powerwall render, with aluminium flashings and trims.

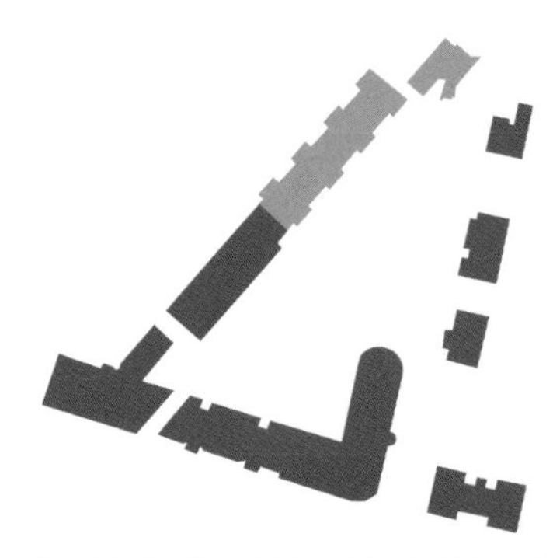

The terraced townhouses by Scottish practice McKeown Alexander face into the Homes for the Future site, while the garages underneath are accessed from the rear of the buildings. The angled section of their two-part Object Building emphasises the block's prominent position at the northern tip of the site's triangular courtyard.

McKeown Alexander

McKeown Alexander Architects is a relative newcomer in Scottish architectural circles. In 1995, Henry McKeown and Ian Alexander were working at Elder & Cannon Architects by day and designing competition entries at night when they won a competition to convert Glasgow's Henry Wood Hall into new rehearsal facilities for the Royal Scottish National Opera. The £4 million project jump-started the practice. Sadly, the scheme failed to get Lottery backing and so was never built, but by then it was too late to go back – the practice was formed and other commissions were starting to come in.

Today, the bulk of McKeown Alexander's work is housing. In addition to the Homes for the Future project, it has three housing association schemes on the go: a £1 million project at Graham Square in Glasgow's East End; the conversion of an orphanage in Paisley into flats; and another project, just outside Paisley, which combines new-build with some refurbishment work. Like most young practices, it has its fair share of house conversions, although it is becoming increasingly selective about the kind of small projects it takes on. "We're interested in high-spec, well detailed jobs," explains project architect Frank Strathern.

In fact, the practice is on the cusp of leaving the world of house extensions behind and breaking into a rather bigger league. Homes for the Future was an extremely high-profile competition for a practice as young as McKeown Alexander to win. Hard on its heels came the job to carry out a feasibility study considering what to do with the area of industrial dereliction that lines the banks of the Clyde in Glasgow. Meanwhile, a commission to refurbish two offices in London for public relations company Biggart Donald looks like helping the practice break out of the purely Scottish market.

Yet despite their ever-increasing number of built projects, McKeown Alexander's style isn't easy to define. Certainly it is modern, both in ambition and appearance. "We believe that new architecture should be challenging and should aspire to progressing our nation's architectural culture," the pair explain. And yet beyond these loose themes, the work changes with each project.

Rather than stylistic traits, the practice prefers to stress its approach to work which blends the avant-gardism that comes from teaching with a good-sized dollop of pragmatism. Somehow McKeown and Alexander both find time to teach (part-time) at the Mackintosh School of Architecture, as well as further afield. The injection of new ideas and questions that this brings to their designs is vitally important and yet they are keen to stress that theirs is a realistic architecture: "We have no preconceptions about architecture nor are we interested in issues of architectural style," they say. "We assert that full integration of structure, programme and context provide the core architectural ingredients of good design." It is what you do with the ingredients, though, that matters. For all their modesty, McKeown Alexander is a practice with a bright future.

McKeown Alexander's terrace is made up of two different types of houses, with either two or three bedrooms. These light, flexible homes with gardens and garages are an innovative and practical solution for family living.

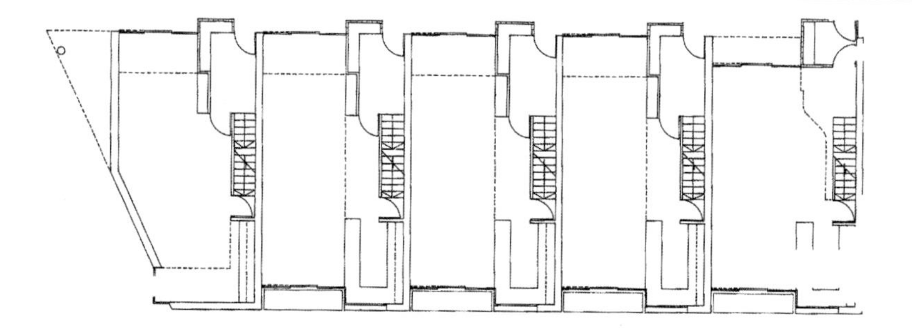

With their full-height windows, the townhouses of Terrace One and the flats in the neighbouring Object Building were designed to make the most of the available light.

The Burrell Company's brief to architects McKeown Alexander was to design a building "which sits on the perimeter of the site, vehicles to the rear, gardens to the fore, thus suggesting medium and larger-scale houses with internal spaces that offer a variety of uses: studies, home/office, studio, etc., with garages beneath."

The architects' design creates a terrace of eight houses constructed from two basic forms. "The terrace is composed of four 'thin' and four 'fat' family homes. Priority is given to enhancing light and volume in living areas by using large-screen windows on the elevation," say the architects. The 'thin' structures are two-bedroom townhouses, while the 'fat' ones are three-bedroom townhouses.

Similar to the Object Building, the structure of Terrace One consists of cavity wall masonry with timber joists, clad with STO render and Ibstock Lodge lane blue brick.

As part of a Glasgow 1999 project which brought together designers, artists and architects to create concept interiors in the Homes for the Future, Konstantin Grcic installed a continuous mantlepiece in the Object Building which can be used to display and store a variety of objects, while design team One Foot Taller developed a modular lounge chair called Ravine.

Developer The Burrell Company commissioned McKeown Alexander to design "a building that would address the pedestrian entrance to the rear of the site yet make the most of its prominent position at the apex of the inner courtyard triangle".

The result has become known as the Object Building because of its position at the northern corner of the site. It consists of seven one-bedroom flats. According to the architects, "it consists of two parts: one linear, the other cranked. Level changes distinguish kitchen and living areas. Large screen windows light the space, providing excellent views."

The structure consists of cavity-wall masonry and pre-cast concrete floors in a concrete frame, clad with STO render, Ibstock Lodge lane blue brick and Western Red Cedar cladding. Windows are made from anodised aluminium and the roof is covered in zinc.

SOLD

Elder and Cannon worked with Rick Mather to create an elevation with a suitably urban scale to overlook Glasgow Green, in which each element was distinctive, but came together in a unified composition. The high-level walkway links the two blocks, across a gap opened up so that glimpses of the Green can be seen from the centre of the development.

Elder & Cannon

Of the seven practices involved in Homes for the Future, Elder & Cannon Architects has possibly the most experience of designing buildings as a catalyst for city-wide urban regeneration.

Set up in 1980, the Glasgow-based firm has rapidly built up a reputation for its urban design work. Just four years in – at the point when most practices are still struggling with small-scale domestic projects – it won the much-coveted job to reconstruct Ingram Square, a rundown block in the heart of Glasgow. Convinced that there was a market for city centre housing if only the accommodation were good enough, the firm's scheme set about converting existing warehouses into apartments and filling vacant sites with new residential and commercial buildings – visit Ingram Square today and you will find it bustling with life.

The practice's combination of architecture and planning skills reflects the experiences of its founding partners, Tom Elder and Dick Cannon. Scottish-born and trained, they both worked in private practice before ending up in the public sector in the 1970s. Elder worked in Glasgow City Council's planning department for several years, during which time he furthered his interest in planning policy and working with historic refurbishment. Cannon, meanwhile, was working as an architect first for Lanark County and then for Strathclyde Regional Council's educational buildings programme. Despite having worked together now for almost 20 years, this breadth of experience still affects the way the practice works.

Elder remains more involved with the refurbishment of listed buildings as well as the general administration of the practice, while Cannon is responsibe for setting overall design standards in the office. The combination obviously works well. Over the years, Elder & Cannon Architects has picked up a string of awards. Most recently, its Moffat Gardens housing, again in Glasgow, was awarded the Glasgow Institute of Architects award.

The firm is very much part of the Glasgow scene; indeed, it has been partly responsible for creating that scene, for helping foster the vibrant design community that we now associate with the city. To this day, the majority of its work is in and around Glasgow. There are occasional forays elsewhere – such as its Blackfriars Street project in Edinburgh or the Kilmarnock bus station – but even then, these are still within the confines of Scotland. The practice is currently completing the first buildings – a primary school and maths and science buildings – for St Aloysius campus in Glasgow.

While the practice is sympathetic to the historic fabric of the city, Elder & Cannon's style is unashamedly contemporary. With its heavily-glazed frontage, render and wood rear elevation, and projecting sky apartment, the design of its Homes for the Future scheme is very much within a European vocabulary of modern architecture that links Glasgow – much as the city was linked at the turn of the century – with architectural developments across the continent.

Previous pages: Penthouse apartment in Elder & Cannon's block, with installation by Adrian Wiszniewski. Opposite: the block is a pivot, connecting the terrace overlooking Glasgow Green with a lower terrace which runs at right angles to it.

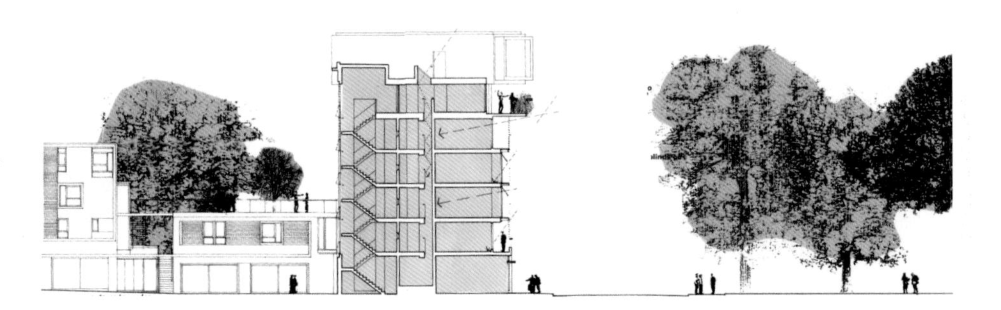

80

Glasgow designers lwd were responsible for the furniture used in the installation (above). Elder & Cannon's building turns the corner with a tight curve, clad in timber. Opposite: the architects also designed a room as part of the "Picture This – design that" project.

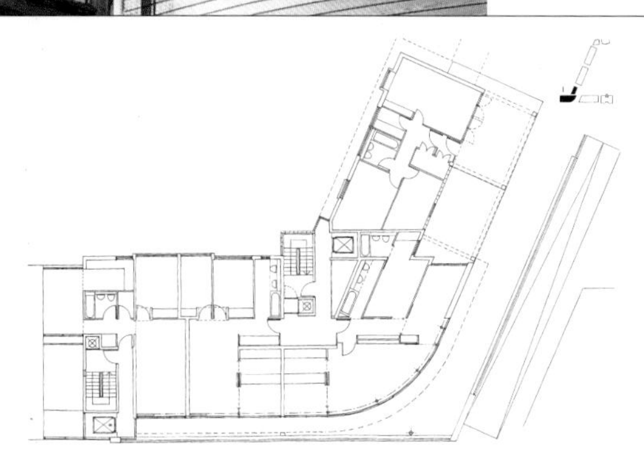

One of the four apartment blocks facing onto Glasgow Green to the south of the Homes for the Future site, John Dickie's Grand Apartments are designed by Elder & Cannon to maximise the benefits of the south-facing position. "The building responds to its parkside setting. The opportunities for maximum light and view are modified with devices to permit shading and privacy," say the architects.

"Here, we wanted to create landmark buildings, with innovative forward-looking designs that responded to and enhanced the area," states Dickie, and the resulting building boasts two two-bedroom penthouses (known as 'sky flats'). Underneath, the building houses four one-bedroom flats, four two-bedroom flats and three flats with three bedrooms. A fifth-storey 'skydeck' links it to the adjoining building by Rick Mather Architects, providing a large platform linking the penthouse apartments on both buildings.

The view between the Grand Apartments and the Mather building to the courtyard beyond is opened up by a curved, cedar-clad wall. This deviation from the building's rhomboid footprint also opens up the space for a first-floor balcony.

Like Elder & Cannon's adjoining terrace building, the Grand Apartments are constructed from blockwork constructed around a concrete frame, with curtain walling, cedar cladding and STO render.

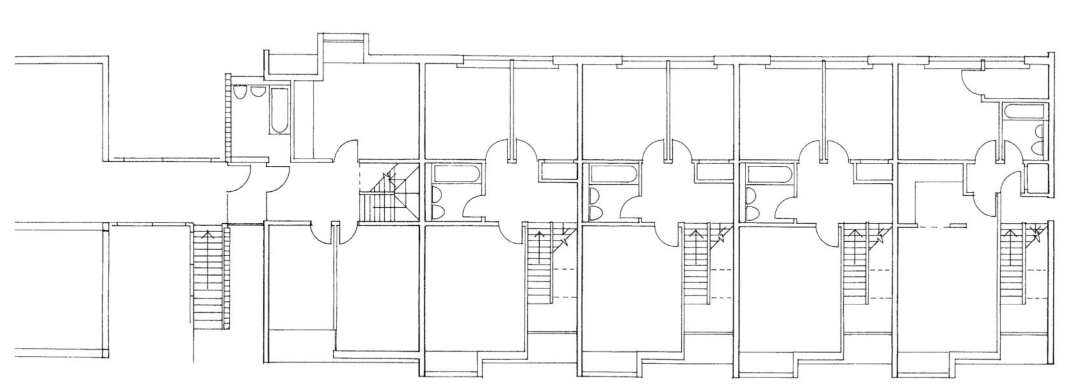

Artist Adrian Wiszniewski's contribution to Glasgow 1999's concept interiors project was a rug based on his paintings (above). While the Grand Apartments have views over the Green to the south (above), the building's rear elevation (opposite) towards the adjoining Terrace Townhouses has much smaller windows. The Townhouses (overleaf) face the site's inner courtyard.

Continuing southwards from McKeown Alexander's adjoining Terrace One, developer John Dickie focused on "trying to provide attractive living spaces along with excellent value for money". Dickie commissioned Elder & Cannon Architects to design this building along with a larger one on the south side of the site.

The terrace structure includes a variety of living units ranging from eight one-bedroom flats and a two-bedroom amenity house, through to two duplex flats with three bedrooms and a five/six-bedroom town house. "These are composed elevations, behind which lie a range of uses," say the architects. "Glazed stairwells engage and enliven the garden courtyard, and hence the route to the Green."

The Terrace Townhouses are linked to the larger, adjacent building via a raised walkway.

The concrete-framed building is clad with STO render and Western Red Cedar, as well as curtain walling.

Rick Mather's building facing the Green has a boldly modelled, sculptured facade, achieved with maximum economy of means. Below the walkway, the perforated steel balconies ripple in and out, while the penthouses opening off the walkway use a more conventional geometry.

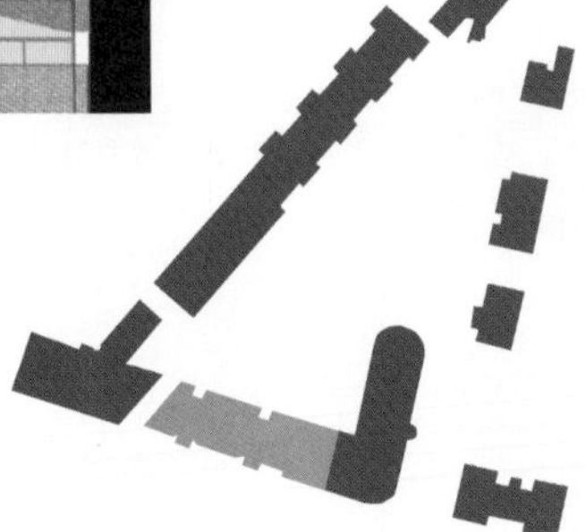

Rick Mather

this way

Homes for the Future brings Rick Mather full circle. When the ebullient American moved to Britain in the early 1960s, one of his first jobs was in the architects' department at the London Borough of Southwark, designing new council housing for slum-cleared areas. A few years later, he and fellow American Don Genasci won surprise third place (there were 350 entrants) in a high-profile international competition for Espoo in Finland with an elegantly conceived scheme in which banks of high-density housing gradually fanned out into the landscape. And yet, since he set up his own practice in London's Camden Town in 1973, Mather has focused on areas other than housing – until now.

Despite being its first housing scheme, Rick Mather Architects' design for Homes for the Future is a logical progression from its work over the past 20 years or so. Mather has always been interested in homes; in creating delightful light-filled places to live in, in (generally) urban environments. Among his first solo projects were two Victorian houses that he refurbished for himself. Turning them upside down – putting the bedrooms on the lower levels – and adding roof terraces, he created living spaces full of light and greenery, with views over the city. Since then, the practice has built up a reputation for its houses. With their crisp forms, white rendered finishes and use of technology — large expanses of glass are a common feature — these bear many of the trappings of Modernism, and yet they are altogether softer too; a response to both the needs of the client and the city as a whole.

To the houses has gradually been added a wider range of work. One of the practice's largest projects in the late 1980s and early 1990s was at the University of East Anglia in Norwich, where it designed a new drama centre and student accommodation. The advent of the Lottery has also seen it moving increasingly into the arts world. This year it will complete a triumvirate of major refurbishment projects in London – at the National Maritime Museum in Greenwich, the Wallace Collection and the Dulwich Picture Gallery.

Its biggest project by far, however, is the commission to masterplan London's South Bank arts complex, a project won in competition against a range of internationally-known architects including Rem Koolhaas, Zaha Hadid and Michael Hopkins. The multi-million pound redevelopment scheme will not be unveiled until later in the year, but the project clearly combines the practice's arts experience with Mathers' long-standing interest in masterplanning.

Homes for the Future similarly brings together the different strands that run through the practice's work: like Espoo and the South Bank, it is about creating a dense new urban environment; like Mather's houses, it is about making spaces in which people feel comfortable and from where they can enjoy city life. Clad in white render, with balconies and big windows, the scheme typifies the practice's 'soft-Modern' approach to design.

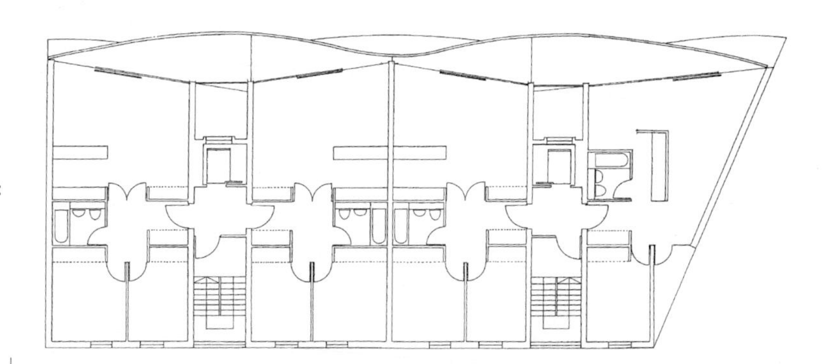

Mather's building links at high level with Elder & Cannon's, and on the street with Ushida Findlay's. It addresses the scale of the setting, essentially urban rather than suburban. On each staircase, there are just two apartments per floor.

James Irving designed a concept interior for Rick Mather's building (right). The structure links at high level with Elder & Cannon's, and on the street with Ushida Findlay's (far right). It addresses the scale of the setting, essentially urban rather than suburban.

Completing the circle around the inner courtyard, and set between Ushida Findlay's Flagship building and Elder & Cannon's Grand Apartments, John Dickie's second large parkfront site is the venue for Rick Mather Architects' contribution to Homes for the Future. "These had to be important, 'city' buildings for the edge of Glasgow Green. They were also designed to be built quickly and efficiently," say Dickie, and the northern, courtyard-facing façade of the building betrays this simplicity of construction with its flat, white-rendered wall. On the other hand, the south façade, with its views over Glasgow Green, employs a more complex alternating wave pattern to create a series of small balconies at every level.

The building is large enough to accommodate six one-bedroom flats and fourteen two-bedroom flats, as well as a two-bedroom duplex flat and three duplex flats with three bedrooms.

Constructed around a concrete frame, the building is made from blockwork with STO render, and curtain walling.

WINE BAR
/ BISTRO
FOR SALE
/ LEASE
GVA Grimley
0870 900 89 90

Architects

The Flagship Building
Ushida Findlay architects

Developer
The Burrell Company
Structural engineers
Dewhurst Macfarlane and Partners
M&E consultants
Fulcrum
QS
The Keillor Laurie Martin Partnership
Planning supervisor
The Keillor Laurie Martin Partnership
Main contractor
Ballast Wiltshier
Sub-contractors
Systems Aluminium Ltd, Nethan Valley, A C White
Sponsors
Lochside joinery, Farside joinery, CTD Ltd, Armitage Shanks Ltd, Keyline Construction, Fine Art Commission, Tradestyle cabinets, Robertson's Interiors, Classique Flooring, Ibstock, Caradon MK Electrics, Concorde Lighting, Hudevad Radiators, Westfield Joinery, Alpha Boilers, Springvale, Potterton Puma plc, Portcullis Door Components, Mr render-Alumasc, Aqualisa Showers, NTL CableTel, Somfy Blinds, Miller Specialist, Sucoflex Roofing, Alpha Ocean Boilers

The Gateway Building
Ian Ritchie

Developer
Thenew Housing Association
Engineers
Arup
M&E Consultants
Arup
Acoustic Consultants
Arup
QS
Davis Langdon & Everest
Planning Supervisor
Housing Association Property Mutual
Main Contractor
Dickie
Clerk of Works
Clerk of Works Inspection Services
Sponsors
Housing Association Property Manual, Dunfermline Building Society, Bank of Scotland, Schuco, Anderson Waterproofing, David Hislop Ltd, Westfield Sawmills, Scottish Power Contracting Services

Wren Rutherford ASL

Developer
Mactaggart & Mickel Ltd.
Interior Designers
Anne McKevitt (triplex flat)
Anusas & MacDonald (barrier-free flat)
Landscape Consultant
Turnbull Jeffrey Partnership
Engineers
Wren & Bell
Planning Supervisor
Mactaggart & Mickel Ltd
Main Contractor
Mactaggart & Mickel Ltd
Site Agent
Jim Jamieson
Sponsors
Allma Construction, Anne McKevitt Design, Behar Carpets, Blairs of Scotland, Brechin Tindall Oatts, Joseph Bell & Sons, P & A Electrical, Ridgewood Roofing, Roxburghe Windows and Doors, Timbmet Woyka Norman, Tradestyle Cabinets, A & D Sutherland, Abigail Banyard, Alexanders' Sawmills, Alumasc, Amtico, Ana Scotland, Apple Macintosh, Airmailed Glass, Ausfern Nurseries, ATAG UK Ltd, Avista (Scotland), Barnaby, BBC, Belysnings Bolaget, Between the Sheets, Bisque Radiators, Bite Communications, BOBO Designs, British Gypsum, Caradon MK Electric Ltd., C & D Tiling, Civil Engineering Developments Ltd, Clayton Munroe, Clifton Nurseries, Concord Sylvannia, Craig & Rose, Crescent Lighting, Crown Paints, Cuthbertson Industries Ltd, DNA Interior Textiles, D Caldwell & Partners, Dartington Crystal, Delta Lighting, DF Wishart, Dorma, Dulux, Eclectics, Elizabeth Hirons, Empire Stores Ltd, Evergreen Exterior Services Ltd, Focus Ceramics, Fanny Blackburn, Frank Farci, Fusion Glass, Gibson & Goold, Glasgow Brickyard, Glasgow College of Building and Printing, Glasgow Education Business Partnership, Graham, Greens Nurseries, Greenberg Glass, H & R Johnston Tiles, Habitat UK Ltd, Hikaru Noguchi, Hitsch Mylius, House, ICI Acrylics, Ideal Standard, Ikea, Jewson, John Richmond, Jon Butcher Designs, Karen Smith, Karol Wilson, Katy Holford, Keith Fuller, Kirkstone Quarries Ltd, Lakeland Limited, Linda Ainsworth, Lush Soaps, Luxcrete, Malcolm Insulations, Marley Thermalite, Michael Sodeau Partnership, Mintec Corporation, Muji, NHBC, Nielsen McNally, Nigel Ross Designs, Noble Russel, Northern Feather Home Furnishings Ltd, NTL CableTel, Ogilvie, Original Bathrooms, Osma Wavin, Pallam Precast Ltd, Paperchase, Parker Knoll Wall Fabrics, Phil Taylor, Philips, Pilkingtons, Plumb Center, Potterson Myson Heating, Premdor, QD Plastics, Raeburn Brick Ltd, Redland Roofing Systems Ltd, Redman Fisher Engineering, Rentokil Tropical Plants, Rugby Joinery, Ruth Perrin, St. James' Primary School, Sacho Hesslein, Salt, Samas Roneo, Sarah Wakefield, Screwy Loos, Sculpture and Design, Sheffield Insulations, Shopkit, South West Acrylics, Spiral Staircase Systems, Sterling Precast, Stylus Graphics, Tapoff Ltd, Targetti Lighting, Tarmac Topmix, Teviot Water Gardens, The Unnatural Light Co, Thistletex Towels, Vacuduct Ltd, Vaillant, Velux, Wainman, Walker Timber Ltd, Weiming Furniture Co Ltd., Windmill Aggregates, Worcester Bosch Thermotechnik, X-film UK Ltd.

Introvert/ Extrovert Building RMJM

Developer
Logan Construction Management Limited
Engineers
The Structural Partnership
Energy Consultants
Lesley Logan, with Caradon and Remcon
QS
Campbell Martin Associates
Planning Supervisor
The Structural Partnership
Main Contractor
Riverbrae Construction Ltd
Sub-Contractors
Nethan Valley
Contractor Team
Gordon Cousins, Angus McLeod, Gary Paterson, John Herbert
Sub-contractors
Nethan Valley Timber Frames, Moore's Kitchens, Thorn Lighting, Caradon Plumbing Solutions, GP Plantscape, Powerwall, AM Electrical & Building Services
Sponsors
Caradon Plumbing Solutions, Somfy Motorised Blinds, GP Plantscape, Moore's Kitchens, Thorn Lighting
Access Technology, Altro Floors, Anderson Roofing, Blu, Brechin Tindall Oats Solicitors, British Gypsum, NTL CableTel, Corian, Clydesdale Bank plc, Eternet, Forsyth Glazing, Home Control, Kirkstone Quarries, Linn Products, Miller Reprographics, Moore's Furniture Group, Pilkington Glass, Porcelanosa, Powerwall, Realstone, Remcon, SMEG UK, Thermal Economics, Vola, Zanussi

Terrace One McKeown Alexander

Developers
The Burrell Company, John Dickie Developments
Engineers
Ove Arup, Blyth and Blyth
M&E Consultants
Max Fordham and Partners
QS
Keillor Laurie Martin Partnership, W.A.B. Brown
Planning supervisor
Keillor Laurie Martin Partnership
Main contractor
Ballast Wiltshier, Dickie
Sub-contractors
Kvaerner, Burnside, Hillhouse Precast, Lochpark Builders, Scotcem, James Cowie, GKN, Maxxiom Power, Seal-Rite, Parkhead Welding, Bute Blacksmiths, Miller Roofing, AC Whyte, Clark & Pearson, D Campbell, Roofseam, D Kennedy, Tradestyle Kitchens, Portcullis, Andrew P Orr, CJ Tiling, Caledonian Sealants
Senior site manager
Brian Murray
Contracts manager
Joe McFarlan
Project Manager
Danny McKibbens
Sponsors
Lochside joinery, Farside joinery, CTD Ltd, Armitage Shanks Ltd, Keyline Construction, Fine Art Commission, Tradestyle Cabinets, Robertson's Interiors, Classique Flooring, Ibstock, Caradon MK Electrics, Concorde Lighting, Hudevad Radiators, Westfield Joinery, Alpha Boilers, Springvale, Potterton Puma plc, Portcullis Door Components, Mr render-Alumasc, Aqualisa Showers, NTL CableTel, Somfy Blinds, Miller Specialist, Sucoflex Roofing, Alpha Ocean Boilers
Bank of Scotland, Schuco, Anderson Waterproofing, David Hislop Ltd, Westfield Sawmills, Scottish Power Contracting Services

The Grand Apartments Elder & Cannon

Architect
Elder & Cannon
Developer
John Dickie Developments
Engineers
Blyth and Blyth
M&E consultants
Max Fordham and Partners
QS
W.A.B. Brown
Main contractor
Dickie
Project manager
Danny McKibbens
Sponsors
Bank of Scotland, Schuco, Anderson Waterproofing, David Hislop Ltd, Westfield Sawmills, Scottish Power Contracting Services

Rick Mather

Developer
John Dickie Developments
Engineers
Blyth and Blyth
M&E Consultants
Max Fordham and Partners
QS
W.A.B. Brown
Main Contractor
Dickie
Project Manager
Danny McKibbens
Sponsors
Bank of Scotland, Schuco, Anderson Waterproofing, David Hislop Ltd, Westfield Sawmills, Scottish Power Contracting Services

Glasgow 1999
UK City of Architecture and Design

GLASGOW 1999 MANAGEMENT TEAM

Deyan Sudjic
Director
Eleanor McAllister
Depute Director
Nicole Bellamy
Exhibitions Director
Pauline Gallacher
Community Initiatives Director
Sarah Gaventa
Communications Director
Andrew Gibb
Development Director
Gordon Ritchie
Marketing Manager
Susan Scott
Establishment Manager
Anne Wallace
Education Officer
Bruce Wood
Glasgow Collection Director

HOMES FOR THE FUTURE CORE GROUP

Deyan Sudjic
Director, Glasgow 1999
Eleanor McAllister
Depute Director, Glasgow 1999
Norrie Innes
Rock DCM
David Page
Page & Park Architects
Hunter Reid
Scottish Homes
Brian Fitch
Glasgow Development Agency
George Campbell
Glasgow City Council
Ricardo Marini
Glasgow City Council
Tony Hughes
Glasgow City Council
Peter Downing
Glasgow City Council

Vincent Wang
Feasibility Studies

Steve Tolson
Chestertons
Beth Reilly
Thenew Housing Association
Tom Lister
Joint Mobility Unit

Picture This – design that
curated by Craig Bremner

Pavilion
Ben Kelly Designs